Napa Valley

NAPA VALLEY

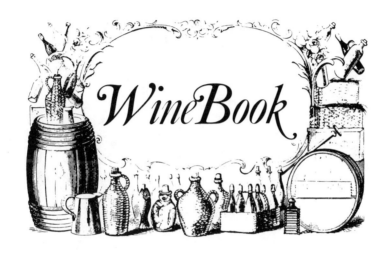

Written by

Richard Paul Hinkle

Illustrations by

Sebastian Titus

A Vintage Image Book

DEDICATION
to
Dr. David M. Kirk (deceased)
Beverly Harris Hinkle

Table of Contents

Looking west across the valley from Howell Mt.

Foreword

oday is part of yesterday and foundation of tomorrow. The glory of Napa Valley wines in their own individual complexity was actually built by several generations of grape growers and vintners, men with pioneering spirits, hard efforts, personal sacrifices and beautiful dreams. Men of different cultures, different origins, they worked hard, step by step solving their daily problems with their own philosophy of "excelsior", upgrading their vineyards, selecting new methods of winemaking, wine aging and wine marketing.

The names of Jacob Schram, Charles Krug, Captain Gustave Niebaum, Georges de Latour, Jacob and Frederick Beringer, Charles Forni, Louis Martini, Elmer and Felix Salmina, Caesar Mondavi and so many others will live forever in Napa Valley history. Some of them, a long time ago, have left this beautiful valley, and some are still living and working together with their children and grandchildren.

As generations of men will come and go, the new generations of vineyards—the new plantings are replacing the old ones, and in centennial life of Napa vineyards, the law of continuous progress eliminates the obsolete varieties of grapes and the new selective vineyards, planted with aristocratic varietals such as Cabernet Sauvignon, Pinot Noir, Chardonnay and few others are opening new horizons for further success, further national and international victories.

Hand in hand with the experimental viticultural work done by University of California, the Napa Valley viticulturist of today pays far more attention to the general ecology, selecting for specific varieties new ecological regimes—new micro-climatic sub-regions of the valley, with proper soil and light exposures, assigning to the new vineyards better managerial techniques—such as formation of vines, pruning, nutritional security and rational qualitative productivity.

This influx to Napa Valley of the new generation of viticulturists is parallel with the new enological initiative of young enologists-winemakers, with their wisdom of conservative progress, granting new ideas and new techniques on the principle of accepting the inheritance of the past.

There is yet so much to do, so much to accomplish and I hope that in the future we never will stop working hard towards the new goals and further achievements, keeping our pioneering ideas not only as a privilege granted us from the past, but as our own duty for a better tomorrow!

Andre Tchelistcheff

East Slope vineyards near Calistoga.

Napa Valley

The Napa Valley is the spiritual center of American winegrowing. It was not the first of America's wine-growing regions, nor is it the largest. But, bestowed with a touch of magic, it has always been the best known.

That Napa's climate is ideally suited to grape growing is unquestioned. That Napa has a long and distinguished history of winegrowing is thoroughly documented. There are many areas which can boast sublime climate and lengthy genealogy. But nowhere else in this country is there the concentration of grape growing and winemaking that exists in the Napa Valley.

Concentration is a function of scale. Slightly more than one half of one percent of California's land area is planted to grapes, and only half of that is in wine grapes. In Monterey County, which has the greatest grape acreage of any coastal county, grape vines account for little more than one percent of the county's land area. In Napa County *five percent* of its rugged, mountainous terrain is planted to carefully selected wine grape varieties. County farm advisor Keith Bowers estimates that fully *four-fifths* of Napa Valley's cultivated land is in grapes!

It is actually getting difficult to keep up with the rapidly increasing number of new wineries in the county. Three-quarters of the bonded wineries in the county are new since 1966, when Robert Mondavi built his winery in Oakville, the first new winery of any size in the valley since Repeal. In 1972 and 1973 a total of 19 new bonds were issued. Nearly a dozen new wineries were bonded in 1978 alone, and that number may well be exceeded in 1979.

Frona Eunice Wait claimed 142 wine cellars for the county in 1889. While it's easy to slight that number by noting that it included every farmer who made wine by the barrel, it seems entirely likely that Napa will again have a hundred wineries, possibly by sometime in the next decade. Be that as it may, with nearly seventy bonded wineries, Napa easily has more wineries than any other county in the country.

As the concentration of grape essences contributes mightily to wine quality, so too does the concentration of winegrowing here contribute to the overall effect. Nowhere is it more evident than in the people who are the Napa Valley winegrowers.

"It's sort of like the Champagne district here," comments farm advisor Bowers, a veteran of thirty years in the valley. "It's a relatively isolated area and the people work closely with one another. These people see each other at church on Sunday, at school functions, at community gatherings, and in the valley's technical group. That closeness fosters a supportive kind of competition, where everyone learns more quickly by their mistakes."

In that last lies another key to Napa Valley's success. The competition here is philosophical, not cut-throat. Those established seem to want the newest wineries to succeed because it benefits the reputation of the Napa Valley as a whole. The competition here is more against an ideal than against one another.

Thus, newcomers are greeted with the warmth of outreaching hands rather than the chill of cold shoulders. Dozens of new wineries assayed their first crush at a neighboring facility. It's practically impossible to visit a new winery without seeing presses and crushers and cooperage that another winery outgrew and was willing to part with for a reasonable price to help out the newcomer.

This spirit of kinship and craftsmanship comes directly from the old West's traditions of barn raisings and quilting bees. It's a spirit that has existed in the valley since the beginning of its winegrowing days, a spirit exemplified by the monumental figure in Napa's early vinous history—Charles Krug.

Krug was *the* pioneer winegrower in the Napa Valley. He used the first mechanical press and built the first commercial winery of any size in the county. It would have been convenient for him to establish a monopoly and shun novices. Instead, he encouraged fresh viticultural industry, generously proffering both time and money to the cause. Jacob Beringer learned winegrowing working under Krug. Carl Wente was Krug's "cellar boss" in the 1870 s. Clarence J. Wetmore (the brother of Cresta Blanca's Charles Wetmore) apprenticed at Krug, as did John C. Weinberger, William W. Lyman, and Emil C. Priber. Frona Wait characterized Krug as "a man whose name has been associated with every venture for the promotion of the industry throughout the State, from its inception to the present, giving a lifetime and a fortune to the work." All true, for Krug died in debt, his life's work ravaged by phylloxera, but not forgotten.

Krug's spirit has outlived him by plenty. You don't have to look far today to find wineries that serve as virtual graduate schools of enology. It's no accident that all of these are among the highest rank of wine producers.

Lee Stewart of Souverain and Fred McCrea of Stony Hill were early boosters of the industry in the fifties. Names like Tchelistcheff, Peterson, Rosenbrand, Heitz, and Grgich came out of the Beaulieu tradition. Freemark Abbey and Joseph Phelps wineries have regular apprenticeship programs for young winemakers, and many an aspiring winemaker has labored in the cellars of Joe Heitz, Mayacamas, or Robert Mondavi prior to opening his own winery.

It is Mondavi who most neatly fits the Krug mold, challenging his comrades to reach for higher levels of winemaking, constantly experimenting, and always providing inspiration and encouragement to the hesitant and unsure. (Is it a coincidence that Robert spent most of his early years at the Krug Winery, where the pioneer's ghost may have been looking down approvingly?)

Greg Bissonette, the personable owner of Chateau Chevalier, was one of those encouraged by Robert Mondavi. "The winemakers in this valley are not in competition *against* each other, but rather *with* each other," he says. "People like Robert and Michael Mondavi, Louis Martini, and many others have been extremely helpful to us, giving freely of their knowledge, lending us equipment, and so forth. Michael Mondavi, for example, spent a lot of time with me just going over cost estimates, projections, and the like."

It was Napa's enticing climate that caused the valley's early inhabitants to consider grape culture. Rainfall averages 25 to 33 inches per year and summer temperatures are routinely in the 80's and 90's. The growing season is well over 200 days, long enough to mature the most stubborn of Cabernet Sauvignons.

Displaying more than a touch of pride, Charles Krug explained to an historian of his time why Napa Valley wines were superior to European wines: "This climate is perfect; the grape ripens fully every year. There are no early frosts, as in France and Germany, to hasten the picking. Our vineyardists manage the picking and pressing of the grapes, and the earlier fermentation of the wine, more clearly, intelligently and skillfully than in Europe. Also . . . better casks are used and the cellars here are almost always above ground, owing to the evenness of the temperature; and [the wines] are clearer and sweeter, and the whole treatment is better."

Weather watchers divide the county into four climatic zones. The region south of Napa falls into the *maritime* classification. The San Pablo Bay narrows the range between day and night temperatures. It also lessens seasonal changes. Summer fogs are common and the growing season shorter. The Carneros district is thus the coolest of the Napa microclimates and is best suited for the earliest ripening varieties. So Chardonnay, Pinot Noir, and Gewurztraminer are the primary varieties planted to the shallow, unyielding soils of the district named for the sheep that once populated its gentle hills.

Andre Tchelistcheff talked about the marked differences between Carneros and the warmer upper valley: "We can have 110 degree summer days in the upper Napa Valley and the temperature can drop 40 to 44 degrees in eight hours. It is the place for the Cabernet Sauvignon and the Sauvignon Blanc. They can take a beating. In the Carneros the high seldom exceeds 90 and an eight hour drop not more than 32 degrees. It is suitable for sensitive, feminine varieties."

The second climatic zone is the *coastal* zone. It is delineated as running from north of Napa to about Lodi Lane (just north of St. Helena). As with the valley as a whole, this region is progressively warmer the farther north of the Bay. Fog usually stops at Yountville, and this region is considered suitable for both early and late ripening varieties. There is little question that some of the world's finest Cabernets are grown in and around Rutherford, though you can easily get an argument as to just how far the mythical "Rutherford dust" extends.

North of Lodi Lane and on into Calistoga the climate is classified as *transitional*. Distinctively warmer than its opposite, Carneros (as pointed out by Mr. Tchelistcheff), the Calistoga area shows off Petite Sirah and Zinfandel, though many other varieties are grown there as well.

Pope Valley and Chiles Valley represent the *interior* zone because their weather patterns are dominated by the continental air mass. Of all the county's climate zones, this is the least influenced by the Bay or the Pacific Ocean. As in Calistoga, Petite Sirah and Zinfandel do quite well, but there is generally less tolerance for other varieties. Still, there are pockets. Cabernet Sauvignon, Chenin Blanc, and Sauvignon

Blanc seem to fare quite well indeed in Chiles Valley. Thermograph readings have shown that some areas of Pope Valley are not nearly as hot as has commonly been accepted, so growers there are trying some Chardonnay and Semillon. The learning never ceases.

As important as climate is, there are many other factors that have to be considered, including exposure, drainage, elevation, and soil. Soils are vitally important.

Most Napa Valley soils are ideal for the support of the culture of the grape. They are generally high in mineral content and well-drained. The latter is essential, as grape vines do not like "wet feet."

Much of the upper valley shows the area's volcanic history in its soils. Rhyolite, basalt, and other volcanic rocks are omnipresent, the result of the eruptions of Mt. St. Helena and other volcanic cones millions of years ago. Volcanic materials are also rich in calcium and sodium, which are beneficial to grape vines.

The lower valley, from the entry of Conn Creek south, shows increasing amounts of sedimentary, acidic, and igneous materials, also beneficial for grape growing. Much of the valley floor is covered with the deep sediment and gravel deposited by the Napa River and its tributaries. This alluvial soil is rich in minerals and provides excellent drainage.

That said, many growers are heading for the hills in hopes of producing grapes with intensely concentrated fruit and flavor, for which they will receive a bonus to compensate for their decreased production. "Even in the better districts," noted Frank Schoonmaker and Tom Marvel (in 1941), "the climate tends to be too warm, and the cooler upland vineyards should there-fore produce better wine than the vineyards in the valleys or along the lower slopes."

As it has taken centuries for European winegrowing areas to discover which varieties best fit, so has it taken decades to begin to determine the proper varieties for each region within the Napa Valley. Forty years ago the leading varieties in the valley were Petite Sirah, Zinfandel, Black Malvoisie (also called Hermitage), and Palomino (or Golden Chasselas). The first two are still widely planted in the valley (Zinfandel is third among reds; Petite Sirah fifth), but the others are almost extinct.

Today Cabernet Sauvignon dominates the valley. Over 5500 acres of Cabernet are planted in the county, and the variety accounted for nearly 30% of the entire 1978 crush!

An indication of the selectivity of grape varieties in the valley today, the preliminary crush report for 1978 showed the first seven varieties accounting for 75% of the entire crush. Those varieties are, in order, Cabernet Sauvignon, Pinot Noir (including Gamay Beaujolais), White Riesling, Chenin Blanc, Chardonnay, Napa Gamay, and Zinfandel.

It is fascinating to learn how important grape growing is to the county as a whole. As important as the Livermore Valley is to California winegrowing, for example, wine grapes typically produce less than 5% of Alameda County's agricultural revenues. In neighboring Sonoma County, wine grapes bring in about half of agriculture's dollars. But in Napa, the figure is typically closer to 90%! In round numbers, over 70,000 tons (a record) of grapes were worth nearly forty million dollars in 1978.

The old Bale Mill north of St. Helena.

The Yount Years

The Napa Indians were one of the "Digger" tribes, so named for their diet, which consisted mainly of roots, seeds, worms, grasshoppers, and fish. The two syllable name is a simple one, easily remembered, though hardly as euphonious as those of other Napa Valley tribes like the Ouluke, the Caymus, the Conahomanas, or the Miacomus (also Maia'kma and Mayacamas, meaning "the howl of the mountain lion").

The Miacomus tribe gave their name to the mountain chain that flows south out of Lake County, where it divides the headwaters of the Russian River and those of Clear Lake. At Mount St. Helena the Mayacamas chain splits, enfolding the Napa Valley between its two branches. (Mount St. Helena was called Serro de los Mallacomes before being renamed by Princess Helen Gagarin, wife of the Russian Governor of Siberia and the Pacific Colonies and daughter of the Czar.)

What "napa" meant to the Indians is uncertain. It was a suffix in the names of some tribes, like the Cabanapos and the Habinapas. Some felt that it meant "home," or "homeland." Others opted for "grizzly bear" or "fish" (the Napa River was plentiful with fish). The most popular meaning is "plenty," or "abundant."

There were more than 5000 natives in the valley in the 1830 s, when white men made their first appearance. In less than a decade their numbers were devastated, first by cholera, then by smallpox. One history says that the cholera epidemic in the fall of 1833 "raged with terrible violence among the Indians. So great was the mortality that they were unable either to burn or bury the dead, and the air was filled with the stench of decomposing humanity."

Between pestilence and slaughter, Indians who had lived in the valley for at least 4000 years were virtually eliminated within four decades. Little wonder that one of the Spanish land grants bears the grisly name "Carne Humana" (human flesh).

Ironically, the first white settler in the valley was a firm friend to the Indian, though he had thrice fought in "Indian uprisings" as a young man in Missouri. Born at Dowden Creek, North Carolina, George Calvert Yount was possessed of the wanderlust. In 1826 he sold his farm to pay his debts (caused by an unscrupulous neighbor who held $1000 of Yount's money in "safekeeping"), left his pregnant wife with their two children, and headed for Santa Fe. (Four years later Eliza Yount obtained a divorce decree for desertion.)

In New Mexico Yount trapped beavers and fought in further skirmishes against Indians. He went into a distilling business with a partner. The business was fabulously successful, but his partner was dishonest, and Yount was again parted from well-earned profits.

He moved on to California in 1831, where he learned to trap sea otters and became friendly with a local tribe of Digger Indians. After three seasons of trapping along the Santa Barbara Channel, he traveled north to explore the San Francisco Bay. Helping to repair the Sonoma Mission, he was the first to make shingles in California. While in Sonoma he helped General Mariano Vallejo to fight hostile Indians.

On the 23rd day of March, 1836, Yount obtained the first grant of land from the Mexican government. His Caymus grant totaled nearly 12,000 acres. That fall he built what is considered to have been the first log house in California. A fortified block-house, the ground level was 18 feet square. The second story, 22 feet square, extended over the first level, and sported port holes from which the house could be defended.

The block-house also boasted the first chimney in California, even though Yount's Padre friends warned him that he would grow old with a fire in the house. He did indeed grow old, living beyond his seventy-first birthday.

Yount's only white companion for some time was an old Frenchman who had served under Bonaparte, though half a dozen families of friendly Indians lived nearby. During one encounter with unfriendly Indians, at great risk Yount ordered the Frenchman to unbar the door to admit his Indian neighbors, who were also in peril.

Grizzly bears were quite abundant in those days. Said Yount, "They were everywhere—upon the plains, in the valleys, and on the mountains, venturing even within the camping-grounds, so that I have often killed as many as five or six in one day, and it was not unusual to see fifty or sixty within the twenty-four hours." In countless encounters with grizzlies and Indians, however, Yount was never wounded. He often said that the most difficult fights he ever had were against land commissioners, squatters, and lawyers.

There is little dispute that Yount was the first grape grower in the Napa Valley. He probably planted his first vines and fruit trees in 1838. The California Agricultural Society's Visiting Committee, in 1856, found 800 acres "inclosed, containing a good variety of fruit trees; an old Orchard and Vineyard planted eighteen years ago, was attractive for the great growth and healthy appearance of the trees and vines."

Yount's vineyard was yielding 200 gallons of wine a year by the early 1850 s, and 5000 gallons a year by 1860.

Yount dominated the Napa wine industry's prenatal period. A larger-than-life figure, he dealt fairly with Indians, Mexicans, and Americans. He gave a part of his ranch for a townsite, called Sebastopol in his lifetime. It was renamed in his honor at his death, six months after Lee's surrender to Grant at Appomattox Court House.

His later life is recalled in a county history: "He retained much of the energy and firmness of his youth, and preserved his memory to a remarkable degree to the last, relating incidents which happened years ago as if they occurred but yesterday, even giving the day of the week and month, without the least reference to notes. He was unostentatious and simple in his manner, narrating incidents of the most startling and thrilling nature in which he played a conspicuous part, without betraying arrogance, egotism, or vanity, and fascinated the listener by his easy and simple statement of facts."

As prominent as Yount was, there were others planting vines and making wine, bit by bit setting the stage for an industry that would dominate the valley much as Yount had.

The old Occidental Winery built in 1878.

As early as 1846 Frank E. Kellogg had planted vines three miles north of St. Helena. In two decades he had 20,000 vines and cleared $3000 a year on their yield. The vineyard was later owned by William W. Lyman, who built a small concrete winery in 1871. Lyman also owned the still standing Bale Mill.

Colonel Joseph B. Chiles, a native of Kentucky, settled on the Catacula land grant in 1844 and became a grape grower 14 years later. The valley northeast of Rutherford bears his name, and still has important vinelands.

The famed Oak Grove Wine Cellar was founded by Judge J.H. McCord, a Southerner lured to California by the Gold Rush. His vineyard and winery were at the Bello Station, midway between Rutherford and St. Helena (about where Franciscan Winery stands today).

McCord had about 40 acres of his 100 acre homestead in vines. Some were Missions that may have been planted in the late '40 s, but he also had Burger grapes that yielded up to 15 tons per acre. McCord produced 50,000 gallons a year and his red and white table wines were aged three years before marketing. He also had 10 acres of Lawton blackberries that made a "celebrated brand of blackberry brandy, highly prized for medicinal purposes." And that was well before Prohibition.

California had been a state two years when brothers Simpson and William Thompson started planting vines on the Suscol grant, four miles south of Napa City. In four years (by 1856) they had 8000 vines, including 29 varieties of newly imported European vines. Interestingly, they abandoned their vineyard soon thereafter, stating that their grape quality was "inferior to that grown upon the hill lands higher up in the valley." It is a theme that has been often restated.

John M. Patchett planted a vineyard west of Napa in 1853. Four years later he made the first shipment of wine from the valley, shipping by wagon six casks and 600 bottles of wine. The following year Patchett had his vintage pressed by Charles Krug, who had borrowed a cider press from Agoston Haraszthy, founder of the Buena Vista Winery in Sonoma. It was the first time grapes had been crushed or pressed mechanically in the valley, and the 600 gallons of wine made that year brought Patchett a princely two dollars per gallon.

In 1859 Patchett constructed the first stone cellar in the county. A modest 33x50 foot building, it accommodated 4000 gallons the following year.

In 1856 Joseph W. Osborn was awarded the $40 prize by the Agricultural Society for the best improved farm in California. Osborn had an orchard, a nursery, and a vineyard at Oak Knoll, six miles north of the city of Napa. Of the 9000 vines in his vineyard, a third were European varieties.

George Belden Crane was an unlikely winegrower. Born in Dutchess County, New York, in 1806, he finished high school at age 16 to become a teacher for ten dollars a month and board. He later attended the Medical Department at State University in New York City. He spent five years practicing medicine and surgery in Scioto County, Ohio, before coming around the Horn to California in January of 1853.

Just south of St. Helena Crane bought chaparral land at the mouth of Sulphur Spring Canyon. In 1859 he planted 12 acres to vines. Over the next two years he added another 42 acres, obtaining cuttings from Haraszthy and from Mr. Stock of San Jose (whose father sent the cuttings from Germany). Crane paid $40 per thousand to Stock. One unlabeled variety turned out to be White Riesling, the first to be planted in the county.

Crane was one of the first to plant vines along hillside slopes, rather than on the fertile bottomland in the center of the valley. Said one historian, "He claims the credit of pioneering, at a large expense to himself, the utilizing of worthless land as a politico-economical measure."

Crane had land on both sides of the highway about where the Christian Brothers fermentation cellars and warehouses are today. He had an underground cellar that measured 50x25 feet, a large double building (80x150 feet), and a stone sherry house of two stories (150x40 feet) that stored 60,000 gallons.

In 1866 Crane sold 32.5 tons of grapes at nearly $60 a ton and made 18,700 gallons of wine from the remainder of his harvest. By then he had a hundred acres of grapes and was the second largest grower in the valley.

Never a bashful man, Crane was quoted as saying, "From this vineyard, in 1865, wine was made which connoisseurs, fresh from the winegrowing regions of Europe, have repeatedly sampled, and uniformly agree that they never saw a more promising wine, of the same age, anywhere." But when Crane journeyed to St. Louis and New York City peddling his wines, he met with little more than indifference.

Another man who threw himself into the winegrowing life (among many other lives) was Sam Brannan. Brannan, who hailed from the grape growing area of Painesville, Ohio, had joined the Mormons in New York. An opportunistic young man of Irish ancestry, Brannan edited the Mormon journal that molded Mormon opinion. When Church leaders decided to "flee out of Babylon," the 26 year old Brannan, already an Elder, was picked to lead a party of more than two hundred by ship to California.

Their ship, the *Brooklyn*, arrived in San Francisco (called Yerba Buena until the following year) on the last day of July, 1846. Brannan founded the city's first newspaper and became a leader of the Vigilantes. He also engaged in a variety of business ventures, using Mormon funds as capital, a practice that eventually caused him to be "disfellowshipped" (excommunicated).

Brannan quite literally and deliberately set off the spark that kindled the flames of the Gold Rush. After securing essential supplies that miners would require (at bargain prices), he marched into San Francisco waving a bottle of gold dust and singing out, "Gold! Gold! Gold from the American River!" His fortune was thus secured.

A decade later, after once attempting to conquer the Hawaiian Islands by bluster, Brannan ventured north to purchase one square mile at the place called Hot Springs. While drunk (as the story goes), he vowed to transform the mineral springs and mud baths into the Saratoga of California—only it came out as "the Calistoga of Sarifornia".

Pritchard Hill Vineyards overlooking Lake Hennessey.

A Wine Industry Is Born

The Civil War was a period of painful transition for America. It was a period of sharp transition in Napa Valley winegrowing as well. The charming, homespun ritual of making wine from one's own grapes (from which we obtain the term "winegrowing") was in the process of becoming an industry. In 1856 there were less than 25,000 vines in the county; a decade later there were a million. In 1849 land went for $1.50 an acre; fourteen years later it was $125 an acre.

In 1862 California was governed by Leland Stanford, later a major winegrower in Alameda, Tehama, and Santa Clara counties. The Civil War battles of Shiloh, Manassas, and Antietam were contested and the two ironclads—the *Monitor* and the *Merrimack* (actually renamed *Virginia*)—fought it out at Hampton Roads, Virginia.

Charles Krug was in his second year at St. Helena in 1862 and Jacob Schram was getting ready to begin tunneling into Diamond Mountain. The teacher and the barber were setting the stage for the vinous revolution that was ready to envelop the valley. Napa would soon become the first name of American winegrowing.

Robert Louis Stevenson appeared to have sensed that potential when he visited Schram, later writing in *Silverado Squatters*: "In this wildspot, I did not feel the sacredness of ancient cultivation. It was still raw, it was no Marathon, and no Johannisberg; yet the stirring sunlight, and the growing vines, and the vats and bottles in the cavern, made a pleasant music for the mind. Here, also, earth's cream was being skim-med and garnered; and the London customers can taste, such as it is, the tang of the earth in this green valley."

Another traveler of the day, unnamed, described the fruitful valley thusly: "The mountains, which form the boundary line on the east and west, are intersected by canyons, which have been rendered very productive. The mountain land greatly enhances the beauty of the scenery. It is covered with magnificent foliage—trees of numberless varieties. Among them are conspicuous the oak, madrono, cedar, fir, and pine. The banks of all the mountain streams are fringed with the willow, the ash, gigantic brakes [tall ferns], flowering manzanita, and the California laurel. Descending into the valley we find an infinite variety of oaks, and here and there clumps of the stately madrono."

The green valley Stevenson described was to be made the more fruitful by the presence of Hamilton Walker Crabb, a native of Ohio who settled in Oakville in 1865. A few years later he purchased a 240 acre tract just south and west of Oakville and began planting wine grapes. The estate eventually ran better than 500 acres, of which 360 were planted to wine grapes.

Crabb evidently brought a rare combination of wit and scholarship to his enterprise. He called his vineyard To Kalon (also written as Tokalon later). In Greek, he would tell Frona Wait, To Kalon means the highest beauty, or the highest good, "but I try to make it mean the boss vineyard." In his "boss vineyard," Crabb began as early as 1874 collecting and planting every variety of grape he could lay his hands on. By 1876 he had planted 183 different varieties and eventually had over 400 varieties under cultivation. It was reputed to have been the largest such collection anywhere.

Crabb's experimental nature paid off when the root louse *phylloxera* began spreading through the north coast during the dry seasons of 1882 and 1883. His research helped to discover that native American root stocks, which had lived with the phylloxera for thousands of years, could resist the damaging aphid.

It is only with the perspective of nearly a century that we can see the progress that phylloxera necessitated: it eliminated the coarse Mission variety, checked the overproduction that threatened financial ruin of itself, it caused the amateurs to abandon their poorly tended vineyards, and brought the State Board of Vinicultural Commissioners into being. Crabb served four years on that Commission.

Crabb, whose closely cropped hair provided a sharp contrast to his grizzled beard, was not only a researcher, but a practical winegrower as well. He built a "plain and unpretentious" winery that was "scrupulously clean" in 1872. In 1880 he produced 300,000 gallons of wine, more than anyone else in the valley (Krug was a close second, at 280,000 gallons). Like Krug, Crabb was happy to share his findings with others. In all, he sold over a million vine cuttings to other growers. To Kalon was known all over the country for its Burgundy, made from "Crabb's Black Burgundy" grapes, which were actually the Refosco of northern Italy (also called Mondeuse).

Crabb died of apoplexy in 1899, but the essence of his life is still present at To Kalon. Portions of his vineyard are still operated as experimental stations by U.C. Davis.

With winegrowing still in its infancy, it is hard to imagine that taxes on wine were much of a burden. Yet J. Ross Browne, the noted Western humorist who lived in Oakland, apparently thought it was so. In June of 1866 he wrote the following in a letter to the Honorable James A. Garfield (then a congressman from Ohio, later President of the United States): "Why, Sir, it would be murder in the first degree to strangle this infant giant of temperance [the wine industry], now innocently disporting himself in his cradle. Tax crinoline if you please; tax the light of woman's eye; tax the light of other days; tax your own ingenuity; tax human forbearance; tax Patience sitting on a monument smiling at Grief; tax wax, hacks, sacks, backs, tacks; tack a tax on attacks on tax; but don't, I beseech you, tax such a beverage as this—the generous grape—with which you may be shot every day of your life, yet never hurt."

In 1866 General Erasmus D. Keyes planted vines on Sulphur Springs Road about a mile and a half west of St. Helena (next to Dr. Crane). Keyes, a former Indian fighter who had been the first commander of San Francisco's Presidio, built a substantial winery the following year. Called Edge Hill, it was one of the earliest stone wineries of any size in the area.

Edge Hill was vastly expanded by subsequent owners, William Scheffler in particular. The winery, which held over a half million gallons at one point, was later sold to a Wall Street broker. "There is probably not a vineyard-home in the State where more money has been used than at Edge Hill, and the improvements are all modern and very substantial in structure," waxed Frona Wait. Today the old stone winery is the comfortable home of Louis and Elizabeth Martini.

In 1870 California became America's leading winegrowing state. Uncle Sam Cellars was founded in downtown Napa and Gottlieb Groezinger bought 800 acres in Yountville, where he later built the large brick winery/distillery that is now the core of the Vintage 1870 complex.

Somewhere around 1872 one W.C. Watson began planting his 70 acre vineyard at Rutherford. He called the winegrowing estate Inglenook, the Scottish term for a cozy corner. By 1879 the estate was producing 154,000 gallons of wine annually. In that year (there is some controversy over this date) the estate was purchased by the meticulous Finnish sea captain, Gustave Niebaum.

Niebaum's reputation painted him as a stern taskmaster, who expected white gloves to remain white through a rigorous inspection of his winery and who would (and did) tear down a distillery in a fury over the remarks of a federal inspector. But Niebaum had a sense of humor, as is evidenced by a story he loved to tell on himself. It seems that Niebaum was walking down one of the lanes of his estate when the commandant of the Veteran's Home (at Yountville) drove up in his horse-drawn buggy. The commandant mistook Niebaum, dressed in an old suit of clothes, as a foreman.

As the commandant had never seen the winery before, he asked Niebaum if he thought his boss would mind if he took a little time to show him around. Niebaum said that he guessed it would be okay with the boss. He guided the commandant around the place. He told the soldier how the boss had changed the course of the creek, which formerly had meandered aimlessly across the fields taking up a great deal of land, and had confined it to a gently curving course between concrete and masonry walls. He also mentioned the white cotton gloved inspection tours.

When the commandant drove Niebaum back to the spot where the two had met, he thanked Niebaum for the tour and gave him a dollar for his pains. The Captain accepted it gravely. Before driving off, the commandant said, "There is just one thing that I forgot to ask you. Who's the ass that's doing all this?" Niebaum replied, "A foreigner by the name of Niebaum."

Jean Adolph Brun, a soldier in the Franco-Prussian War, was a man of many skills. He was a maker of cider, olive oil, and wine. A chemist, he worked in the manufacture of photographic supplies in Canada and Australia before coming to the Napa Valley in 1874.

He produced wine for others around Yountville for a couple of years, carefully saving his money. By 1877 he had saved enough to team up with his grape grower friend and compatriot Jean Chaix. Together they bought a vineyard on Howell Mountain, then built a stucco fronted winery next to the railroad in Oakville. They called their venture Nouveau Medoc and, by 1881, their 34x20 foot winery had been expanded to 34x160 feet. Production jumped from 55,000 gallons a year to

Looking west off Zinfandel Lane.

130,000 gallons. Their specialty was a sweet red wine that, for some reason, was immensely popular in New Orleans.

In 1875 the San Francisco jeweler Charles Lemme built a stone winery above Charles Krug on Spring Mountain. For his trade, Lemme called the 285 acre estate La Perla. His daughter married August Schilling, of the San Francisco family of dealers in wine, spices, coffee, and tea. Schilling later inherited the property. Owned by Jerome Draper Sr., the magnificent estate now covers 435 acres. A hundred acres are in vines, set in steep terraces on the undulating hills. Leon Adams calls the vineyard "one of the most spectacular in the world," and its true splendor can only be fully appreciated from the air.

Winegrowing came to the Napa Valley in a hurry when it came. In 1860 the valley produced just over 8000 gallons of wine. A decade later the figure had jumped to 300,000 gallons, and another decade saw production at around 2.5 million gallons. (By comparison, the valley was producing between five and seven million gallons a year through most of the 1940's and 1950's. In 1978 production was around 12 million gallons off of a record harvest of more than 70,000 tons.)

Frona Eunice Wait, in her book *Wines & Vines of California*, gives us a charming idea of what frost protection was like in the '80 s: "...and if at night there is a tendency toward nipping frosts during the critical month of May an electric barometer close by the bedside of the sleeping vineyardist gives timely warning. Instantly the whole household is astir and soon the bundles of straw placed at intervals throughout the strip of vinelands are ignited, and the high hills help to envelop the valley in a mantle of close, clinging smoke, thus preventing the possibility of frostbitten vines."

The year La Perla was built saw the formation of the St. Helena Viticultural Club. Its first president was, fittingly, Charles Krug, and Hamilton Crabb was one of three vice presidents. The club met twice a month to pool information, particularly regarding phylloxera, which was rapidly becoming a serious problem in Napa as well as in Sonoma, where it was first discovered.

In 1878 the Club erected a brandy warehouse on Church Street (still standing), later expanded, and in 1880 built a two story Viticultural Hall. Membership was well over a hundred by the following year.

The year of the American Centennial found John C. Weinberger building a 150,000 gallon cellar of red lava rock due north of Charles Krug. Weinberger also started a new industry, producing grape syrup at his winery. He had a vineyard of 68 acres.

The same year marked the beginning of the Beringer saga. After purchasing the "old Hudson place" from William Daegner, Jacob Beringer hired Chinese coolies to bore into the steep hillside just off the main road. The cornerstone was laid the following year, as recorded by the *St. Helena Star*: "The center of attraction was the stone itself, neatly chiseled out by Baillie, and appropriately inscribed 'B.B., 1877,' and containing various excavations for the deposits that were to be made therein. These consisted of copies of the *Star* and many cards of persons attending. Professor Smith deposited a photograph, Aug. Tonolla a Hungarian

Los Carneros Vineyards below Milliken Peak.

bank note, and Charles Krug a $20 gold coin. Bottles of native wine and champagne were also interred here for future generations to resurrect and sample. After short speeches Dr. Mitchell baptized the stone with champagne and the cover was lowered to its place."

The sturdy, three story Occidental Winery was built in the Stag's Leap area in 1878 by Terrel Grigsby. Grigsby, who had helped his brother build Mountain View Winery in Yountville earlier, had also helped raise the Bear Flag over Sonoma during the revolt of 1846.

Cycles of boom and bust are common in agricultural enterprises, and winegrowing has never been immune from them. California wines were popular in the 1870 s. Bismark was fighting Napoleon III in Europe, seriously impeding the export of French wines. High tariffs on imports and the rising tide of European immigration into the U.S. also created a demand for California wines.

Vastly increased plantings, coupled with worldwide depression, brought the bust cycle into maturity in 1876. But by the end of the decade things were on the upswing again. The following decade brought a number of new wineries to the valley, many of which were prodigious structures of stone designed by Hamden W. McIntyre, a Vermonter who was the dominant designer of wineries during the last century.

McIntyre's first two Napa Valley projects were Seneca Ewer's Rutherford Winery (now the central core of the Beaulieu winery) and Captain John Benson's Far Niente Winery, adjoining To Kalon south of Oakville.

Fortune Chevalier came in 1884 to Spring Moun-

tain, where his son George would later supervise the construction of a fairy tale castle winery. Just below Chateau Chevalier was Tiburcio Parrott, confidant to the Beringers and builder of the elegant Parrott House. (Mike Robbins of Spring Mountain Winery now owns Parrott House.) The illegitimate son of the U.S. consul at Mazatlan, Parrott was a patron of the arts, a Spanish gentleman, and a lover of growing things.

When Parrott became interested in olive trees, he had 5000 planted on his 1500 acre Miravalle estate. He grew tobacco, oranges, lemons, and cultivated many rare flowers, shrubs, and trees. He was also a winegrower, and A.R. Morrow once told Leon Adams that Parrott's "Miravalle Margaux" was the greatest wine produced in California prior to Prohibition.

The turn of the century saw the coming of Georges de Latour, and his Beaulieu Vineyard, and Theodore Gier's Sequoia Vineyard and Winery. Sequoia, in the redwood forested foothills west of Napa, had first been planted around 1864 and had once been a popular weekend and summer resort area. Gier would later sell the 338 acre property, with its 300,000 gallon stone winery, to the Christian Brothers.

With the battle of phylloxera safely behind them, the winegrowers of the Napa Valley looked forward to a century of expansion and progress. They refused to believe that the forces of temperance and intolerance were including wine in their tirades against spiritous beverages. Winegrowers went almost up to the very day National Prohibition took effect thinking that they would be exempted from its provisions.

The first stone for Far Niente was laid in the spring

of 1885. Grapes were crushed that fall, and the large stone building was completed the following summer. The name is Italian for "without a care," and Benson's label showed a little girl sleeping in a hammock. Closed by Prohibition, the structure is now owned by grape grower Douglas Stelling, who has already begun to renovate the winery.

In 1886 McIntyre, described as being "uncommonly tall," did the Eshcol Winery (now, as Trefethen Winery, the second oldest wooden winery in the valley) and began work on Inglenook. He completed that the following year, then went on to build Greystone Cellars, the largest stone winery in the world. When he finished Greystone in 1889, he had built the two most enduring and enchanting winemaking fortresses of the Napa Valley. To this day Inglenook and Greystone attract hundreds of thousands of visitors annually, many drawn as much by the grandeur of the structures as by the wines produced therein.

Greystone deserves mention also for the man behind its construction. William Bowers Bourn Jr. was born into a wealthy family in San Francisco. When he finished prep school, he left for England to study at Cambridge. He returned at age 21 to take over the operation of his late father's Empire gold mine in Grass Valley. Though others had thought the mine played out, it remained in operation until 1956, by which time it had produced $70 million worth of the yellow metal.

Bourn was involved in a variety of business interests. Two of his sisters owned vineyards in St. Helena. By the middle '80 s things were very bad for independent growers. They were disorganized and totally at the mercy of the San Francisco merchants for the prices they would receive for their grapes. Bourn, who had a passion for order, decided to build a grand winery that would receive the growers' wines, loan them ten cents a gallon on their wine (the banks would not), and age it for them until it could be sold.

Bourn's partner in the venture was Everett Wise. Their circular, posted in the winery, said: "No Malvoisie, Mission, inferior grapes, or grapes in bad condition will be received for wine-making." Their noble and altruistic plan, well thought out from the business point of view, lacked only the knowledge that phylloxera would disrupt their best-laid plans. A half dozen different owners would operate the winery until the Christian Brothers took it over after World War II.

The decade of the 1880 s was a busy one in the Napa Valley. Judge John Stanly planted 100 acres of vines at his La Loma estate in Carneros, a site still marked by a row of giant eucalyptus. The former Lisbon Winery, built in 1882 by Joseph Mathews, is the last surviving native stone winery in the city of Napa. At the northeast corner of Yount and Brown streets, it is soon to be made into a restaurant.

The Napa Valley Wine Company was organized in 1883 by Alfred Tubbs and Charles Krug to sell the wines of Napa Valley growers directly to the retail trade. Most of the growers had previously sold their wines to merchants (*negociants*) who were blending their wines with inferior wines. Growers could now take their grapes to Krug's winery or to Col. John Fry's Vine Cliff Winery in Yountville for vinification. The company then leased a building in San Francisco for their half million gallon (all oak cooperage) aging facltiy.

West Slope seen from Larkmead Lane.

Prohibition Years

It's hard to imagine that the winegrowers of California really didn't know that National Prohibition meant them. Certainly they didn't *want* to believe it. Horatio F. Stoll, writing in the first issue of *California Grape Grower* (later *Wines & Vines*) on December 1, 1919, said: "During the last weeks of August, the writer visited practically every grape district in the State in an effort to arouse the growers to an understanding of the critical situation. He was amazed to find them making absolutely no preparations for the disposal of their crop in case the wineries were not permitted to operate. They turned a deaf ear to the suggestions that they should try to develope other avenues of escape than winemaking."

Some of the alternatives that Stoll suggested were driers (which were expensive), boxing the grapes for fresh shipment, producing grape concentrate, grape syrup, or grape juice. Eventually these "other avenues of escape" would be tried. But only when the winegrowers were finally convinced of the gravity of the situation.

"Lulled into a sense of false security by well-meaning but mistaken friends," Stoll went on, "they announced they were going to make wine, because the ban would surely be lifted before the crop was ready to be harvested."

But National Prohibition was the law of the land, and would be for fourteen years. The arguments for and against would ring with hollow rhetoric throughout Prohibition's duration, but no single piece of oratory grabs the imagination and the humor quite like the statement of the Eighteenth (Prohibition) Amendment's author, Senator Morris Sheppard of Texas: "There is as much chance of repealing the Eighteenth Amendment as there is for a hummingbird to fly to the planet Mars with the Washington Monument tied to its tail." N A S A has no record of the flight.

The press for national prohibition had been around for decades. The Prohibition Party, in fact, had been in existence since 1869, though it never did carry much clout. Prohibition didn't begin to approach political reality, however, until December of 1917, when the Eighteenth Amendment to the Constitution was submitted to the states by Congress. It took hardly more than a year for the needed 36 states to ratify the amendment. Nebraska put Prohibition on the books on January 16, 1919. The enabling legislation—The Volstead Act—was passed by Congress in October, but President Wilson vetoed the measure, which was then passed over his veto a week after the League of Nations held its first meeting at Geneva, Switzerland. Neither effort would stand the test of time.

It was a curious anomaly that Prohibition did not kill the wine business. In fact, grape growers made all the killings during the first seven years of what President Hoover would later defend as "an experiment noble in motive and far-reaching in purpose."

In the Napa Valley, overproduction during the first two years of the century had caused a marked decrease in grape prices. The 1903 crop, due to adverse weather, was short, which brought prices back up. Through the first two decades of the 20th century Napa Valley prices fluctuated between $9.50 and $30.00 a ton. Came Prohibition, the average price jumped to $50 in 1919, $75 in 1920, and $82 per ton the following year. Prices as high as $125 a ton were paid for juice (wine) grapes in the valley during the ignoble experiment.

Much of the demand came from the east, where European immigrants living in metropolitan areas happily returned to the practice of making their own wine. Wine had always been a mealtime beverage to them and they saw no reason to cease having wine on account of a silly law.

Stoll estimated that fully half of California's 1919 crop of 400,000 tons could have been shipped east had there been enough rail cars available. A rail strike complicated matters further, and the crop was exceptionally large. Still, there was a vast increase in the shipment of grapes east.

To further assist the growers, prices were fixed and guaranteed six months in advance. The financial climate was so enticing that grape acreage actually increased in the valley by nearly two thousand acres in the 1920's. (The increase brought Napa's bearing acreage to nearly 11,000 acres. Today's bearing acreage is better than twice that.)

The bubble burst in 1926 when price-fixing was dropped. Prices plummeted to as low as $10 a ton, though the average for the year was $45 per ton. By 1928 that average was down to $25, and a low point was reached in 1932, when Napa Valley grapes sold for an average of $12 a ton. Between Prohibition and the Depression, things looked bleak for winegrowers.

Even when life appeared bleakest in 1932, better days, even happy days, were just around the corner. An ambitious young man, once Secretary of the Navy and Governor of New York, was enthusiastically campaigning for the White House. Included in Franklin Delano Roosevelt's comprehensive programs for reform and recovery was his support for the repeal of Prohibition.

Roosevelt's sweeping victory was perhaps best characterized by Will Rogers, who said, "The little fellow felt that he never had a chance and he dident till November the Eighth. And did he grab it!" It didn't take long for 36 states to ratify the 21st Amendment to the Constitution (repealing the 18th). California ratified in June. When Utah ratified on December 5, 1933, Prohibition was no more than a bad memory.

Good for a time to grape growers, Prohibition had been a near disaster for winemakers. The state had boasted 700 wineries in 1920. Sonoma had 256 of that number, followed by Napa with 120, and Santa Clara with 49. The numbers rapidly depreciated through the twenties. By the end of the decade less than 300 were still maintaining their bonds and, when repeal came in 1933 just 160 of the original 700 were still hanging on.

Fortunately for the survivors, wine had not been forgotten. In fact, more wine was being produced annually by the end of Prohibition than had been made at its outset. American wine production was 45 million gallons in 1919; by 1930 that figure was 150 million gallons, much of it produced in hundreds of thousands of households across the country. "Ironically," said one commentator, "millions of Americans tasted their first glass of wine during the great social experiment to prohibit the commercial sale of alcoholic beverages."

One popular product of the period was the "wine brick." This was nothing more than a 4 by 8 inch block of dried and compressed grapes. It carried the following caution: "Warning: Do not place this Wine Brick in a one-gallon crock, add sugar and water, cover and let stand for seven days, or else an illegal alcoholic beverage will result."

There might have been some uncertainty about the status of home winemaking, but Treasury Secretary Andrew Mellon was quoted as saying, "If any citizen in any part of the United States wants to buy a ton or so of California juice grapes, it is none of a prohibition agent's business."

Charles M. Crawford has, for nearly four decades, been with the Modesto operation of the E. & J. Gallo Winery (which has, incidentally, provided the Napa Valley with winemakers like Dick Peterson, Philip Togni, Brad Webb, Walter Schug, Jerry Luper, and Dimitri Tchelistcheff). Crawford recalled the days of Prohibition: "People ... were tempted to make wine at home and concocted such beverages as dandelion and elderberry wines, or sent away for instant do-it-yourself winemaking kits of wine bricks made of raisins accompanied by yeast and instructions, in order to make a raisin wine. [There was] a remarkable resemblance to the Victorian era of consumer ignorance and

its accompanying acceptance of substandard wine concoctions. People were encouraged, by necessity, to accept bad beverages."

There were wineries that remained open and in production through the legal drought. Georges de Latour was close to San Francisco's Archbishop Patrick Riordan, so Beaulieu produced altar wines for nationwide distribution. Business was so good that de Latour had the Wente Brothers Winery of Livermore bonded as "Beaulieu Vineyard Number Two" to increase his production of sacramental wines. The wily Frenchman also set aside choice red and white table wines for aging, knowing that the madness had to pass, sooner or later.

Before the madness passed, however, many strange concoctions were created to produce alcoholic beverages within the confines of the law. The great euphemism of the day referred to "medicinal wines." Wine and liquor were easily available under a doctor's prescription, and many doctors prescribed wine freely. "One wineglassful with meals" was a common dosage.

Wines, of up to 22% alcohol, could even be purchased without prescription if they were "medicated." Called "tonic" wines, one or more foul-tasting additives would be added to a base wine. Most of these additives, however, could be precipitated out by refrigeration, an early and effective use of cold stabilization. The resulting wine was pure, and occasionally palatable. Garrett's famed "Virginia Dare" was a "tonic prepared with Tokay wine, containing medicaments of Tonic value, scientifically allocated in a menstruum of aged, matured wine. No laxatives or harmful drugs. Especially recommended to convalescents."

Old La Perla Winery atop Spring Mountain.

The madness did pass, but only a few wineries were prepared for business as usual. Beaulieu and Beringer had remained in production throughout the black days, and so were ready with aged table wines. The Christian Brothers. newly moved to Mont La Salle from Martinez, and assured by the cut of their cloth of being able to make at least altar wines, were also ready for Repeal.

One optimist was Frank A. Busse, who filed articles of incorporation for the Napa and Sonoma Wine Company in January of 1933, having "faith in the return of legalized wine." Fortified by the weight of Roosevelt's landslide victory, no doubt. Another winery founded in '33 was the Muther Wine Company. In another era, one might suspect a collegiate play on words, but this outfit, also known as Cluster Grape Products, was owned by Fred E. Muther. In a winery on Spring Street that dated to 1862, Muther's phone number was 196. "Vintners Supreme" was his label.

The Great Depression was still playing when Repeal came, and it was difficult to raise the necessary capital for a new wine business. One way around that was the cooperative, a popular mode of operation throughout California at the time. The Napa Valley Co-op was formed by eight growers in Calistoga in 1934. Now in St. Helena, the winery sells its wine to Gallo and involves over 250 Napa Valley growers.

California winemakers in general, and Napa Valley winemakers in particular, had several hurdles to overcome when Repeal came. Much of the industry's wooden cooperage had been badly kept during Prohibition. Barrels and tanks were full of mold, acids, and bacteria. Upon Repeal, everybody rushed to get into the act, using improperly cleaned cooperage, which yielded wines of high volatile acidity.

Still, there were advantages to be gleaned from the industry's rebirth. Brother Timothy, of The Christian Brothers, considers California's wine industry as practically new since Repeal. "Prohibition damaged and destroyed things that have not been replaced," says Brother Tim, "but after Repeal the whole California wine industry was ready to accept new ideas and techniques. We were not hidebound by tradition, not wedded to the past, nor were we governed by senile thinking. We've been progressive, and we've been extremely eager to listen to the new, scientific ideas from the University of California."

Prices fluctuated wildly at Repeal. In 1934 bulk dessert wine was going for $1.25 a gallon due to its scarcity. Within six months that figure was halved and, after the large 1935 crush, was halved again. From 1936 to 1942 bulk dessert wines ranged from 25¢ to 40¢ per gallon.

Despite the problems of re-creating an industry almost from scratch, the Napa Valley was deliriously happy to be back in business. The four day vintage festival of 1934, held in St. Helena, was dubbed "a credit to Hollywood." Elaborate displays were put up by Beaulieu, the L.M. Martini Grape Products Company, and F. Salmina & Company. Others participating included Beringer Brothers, Bisceglia Brothers (who owned Greystone Cellars at the time), Inglenook, the Lombardi Wine Company, the Madrone Wine Company, and the Napa Valley Cooperative Winery.

Neo-Formative Period

The Napa Valley has long been made special by its people. They have been self-starting, individualistic sorts, people strong enough within to be willing to extend a helping hand to those following their lead. Hardy people were required to supervise the industry's rebirth after Prohibition. Through the thirties the average price of Napa Valley grapes never exceeded $22.10 per ton.

Despite the difficulties inherent in starting over, the Napa Valley maintained its reputation for quality. Said H. F. Stoll, "Some of the finest dry wines in the state are produced in this district. A drive through the beautiful Napa Valley from Napa through St. Helena and up to Calistoga is a revelation."

The California State Fair of 1940 brought numerous awards to the valley. Napa took first in the dry wine sweepstakes and second in the sweet. Golds were garnered by Inglenook's Sauterne, Riesling, and Moselle. Beaulieu won the gold for its Cabernet (no surprise) and Sparkling Moselle; Beringer also won a pair, for Port and Dry Sherry, and F. Salmina's Burgundy also collected a gold. Napa wineries also took the silver and bronze medals in the Cabernet, Riesling, and Burgundy competitions. Beaulieu took the silver in Angelica and Napa wineries had the only awards for Burger, Golden Chasselas, Semillon, Traminer, and Barenblut. (It should be noted that the State Fair then awarded only one of each medal in each class.)

Among the hardy people attracted by the valley was Louis Michael Martini, the square-jawed, resolute Italian who was bound to produce the best in dry wines. Though most of his years had been spent producing sweet wines in the inland valley (sweet wines outsold dry wines by better than two to one in those days), Martini quietly built a model winery just south of St. Helena and went about compiling an inventory of fine table wines. In 1940 he sold his Kingsburg winery, moved his family to St. Helena, and put his entire line of Napa Valley table wines on the market. "At that time when fine California wines were scarce," says Leon Adams, "their quality created a sensation. He became famous overnight as one of the coast counties premium table-wine producers."

While Martini was making the big splash, others were taking a different tack, creating tiny ripples that have only recently become major swells. These individuals were founding the first "boutique" wineries. Almost uniformly, they were men who had been quite successful in other fields, but yearned for the ultimate challenge, the challenge that would bring them into close battle with that "mean old lady" (Joe Heitz' apt phrase) — Mother Nature.

The first of these were Jack and Mary Taylor. An Englishman, Jack had graduated Cambridge and gone to work for the Shell Oil Company. Mary, a music lover and gourmet cook, would later publish two books of rounds and found a seasoning company. In the summer of 1941 the Taylors purchased a ranch on the slopes of Mt. Veeder, west of the city of Napa. Their first job was to pull out a prune orchard, fence its 18 acres, and plant vines along the contours of the natural amphitheatre Jack dubbed "Grape Bowl."

The property had originally been called Mt. Veeder Vineyards, but after hearing the shriek of a mountain lion one night, the Taylors renamed their winegrowing venture Mayacamas (for the Indian word meaning "the howl of the mountain lion").

The Taylors may have established the record for setbacks in their early years. One foreman was killed in a tractor accident and Mary's brother nearly suffered the same fate. A snowstorm and hail held up the surveying of Grape Bowl, rain delayed its planting, and the deer fence (bought and paid for) was held in a warehouse for the duration of the war by the government.

When the Taylors were ready to make their first wine in 1947, a government inspector threatened to withhold their bond. It seemed that they didn't have a proper sign and that one door was held up by hinges sporting two bolts instead of the required three. While Mary painted a legal sign (in watercolors), Jack reworked the hinges while the inspector watched. The effort was for naught, as their first wine suffered, as Mary so delicately puts it, "an unlucky fate."

Despite the seemingly endless intercession of the fates, the Taylors have fond memories of their years on Mt. Veeder. Mary recalls the assistance provided by Ernest and Herman Wente in obtaining Chardonnay budwood: "Most of it was given to us by the generous Wente brothers of Livermore, who offered us as many cuttings as we needed. Mr. Ernest Wente [the vine-yardist of the family] told us he thought we were very foolish to plant nothing but Chardonnay, if we hoped to make a living, because of its low crop yield. But Mr. Herman Wente [the winemaker] encouraged us by saying he thought we had picked the ideal spot to produce a superb wine from that variety and he wished us the best of luck. It was his words we chose to remember, but they were both right."

The indomitable Taylors were not alone in taking on Mother Nature's challenge. The year 1943 brought the Mondavi clan to St. Helena, saw real estate investor Jerome Draper Sr. purchase the 282 acre La Perla vineyard estate on Spring Mountain, and Lee Stewart found his Souverain Winery on Howell Mountain.

Stewart sold his first two vintages off in bulk (to the Mondavis at Krug), but decided to market wine under his own label upon the advice of Andre Tchelistcheff.

"In 1945," recalls Stewart, "Andre Tchelistcheff came up. This was in December. He said, 'These are marvelous wines. Next year you're going to be owning a Cadillac.' Well, instead of owning a Cadillac, for ten years we drove a bloody Pontiac with the springs coming up through the upholstery. And we ate rutabagas."

Rutabagas? "I'm not kidding," Stewart continued. "It was really tough. In January (1946) we had our first wines for sale. Our gross sales for that month were a dollar and a quarter. That was a gallon jug which I sold to the assistant winemaker at Beaulieu. The gross sales for the entire year were twenty-five hundred dollars. We didn't really start to make any good money until about 1965."

World War II brought several disruptive influences to Napa County's premier industry. Shortages of equipment, supplies, and transportation were bad enough, but the shortage of labor was a great hurt.

Yet crisis brought out the best in people. When the vineyards were ripe with fruit, whole businesses would close up so that their employees could spread out into the fields and help bring in the harvest. In 1943 Mexican nationals were brought north to help with the crush, a practice that was continued into the early sixties. Of that first instance, the *St. Helena Star* laconically editorialized, "Mexicans saved our bacon."

Grape prices soared during the war years. The county average jumped to $31 a ton in 1942, then to $78 in '43, and to $111 the following year. By-products of wine helped fill needs that would otherwise have gone unmet. Tartrates, wine vinegar, grape concentrate for flavoring and sweetening, tannic acid, and cream of tartar were items that would have been imported in other times.

The curtailment of imports also gave greater exposure to California wines. The destruction of European vineyards allowed people who might otherwise have never tried California (and Napa Valley) wines to acquire a taste for them. Significant technological growth would also come out of the war years.

The artificially high demand for wine and its by-products bounced grape prices around, by and large keeping them high. The average in Napa Valley dipped to $62.30 a ton in 1945, then jumped to $104 the following year. But that was just a setup for the big fall in late '46 and early '47. Grape prices plummeted to $33.40 a ton, finally reaching a low in 1949 of $29.80. Everybody bought wine in 1946, driving the bulk market up to $1.75 a gallon. In the fall of '46 the price slid to $1.35. The downward trend was dizzying and the summer of '47 saw almost a dollar lopped off the last price: down to 38¢ a gallon.

Grape and wine prices began a modest rebound as the late forties looked toward a new decade. In 1948 California's ballot proposition for statewide Prohibition was defeated. The same year Robert Lawrence Balzer published a book entitled *California's Best Wines*. In listing the state's twelve best wines, Balzer selected four from the Napa Valley: Beaulieu's Private Reserve Cabernet Sauvignon, Inglenook's Gamay, and Louis Martini's Johannisberg Riesling and Dry Sherry.

In 1949 Napa County produced five and a half million gallons of wine, of which all but the half million was dry table wine. Statewide, over seventy percent of the crush was in dessert wines. Four counties produced more wine than Napa.

Even then restaurateurs were taken to task for charging outrageous prices for bottled wine. Irving Marcus, editor of *Wines & Vines*, talked of a customer paying $2.50 a bottle in a restaurant, and then seeing the same wine in a package store for 90¢ or $1.00. "This man is going to feel that he was robbed — and in our opinion, he was."

Still, there were a few restaurateurs willing to keep wine pricing in some perspective. One was the Miramonte Hotel in St. Helena (reopened in 1978). In 1960 owners Basilio and Vanessa Lucchesi offered most of their entrees at less than $2 (the steak dinner was $2.50). They served Napa Valley wines almost exclusively (a few Italian imports were also on the wine list). Lucchesi was choosy about the wines he selected, and priced them all at $1.75 the bottle. "The customer should order his wines from the left rather than from the right-hand column of the wine list," he maintained. "Those who recognize something particularly fine deserve a break."

Leon Brendel opened his winery next door to Louis Martini in 1949. A native of French Alsace, Brendel had studied chemistry in France and Bavaria, organized a school for distillers in Switzerland, been a winemaker in Mexico, and a consultant in southern California before coming to the Napa Valley to work for the Aherns at Freemark Abbey.

Brendel is remembered for operating a winery that produced only one wine, Grignolino, which was sold under Brendel's "Only One" label. "His Grignolino wine is darker in color than most other California Grignolinos and has a distinctive flavor and charm of its own," applauded John Melville. But Brendel was an inventor as well, leaving the industry an electromechanical wine hose cleaning unit and a bench budding gadget that made grafting easier.

Napa wineries did as well at the 1950 State Fair as they had a decade earlier. Beaulieu collected twelve awards, including four golds, four silvers, and the sweepstakes award. Louis Martini also picked up twelve, while Inglenook and Charles Krug each had eleven (the last three earning two golds apiece).

Late 1950 saw the erection by the vintners' group of the redwood colored sign along Highway 29 that said: "Welcome to this world famous wine growing region." The original sign listed the following wineries: Beringer, Martini, Inglenook, Freemark Abbey, Beaulieu, Napa Co-op, Vin Mont, Christian Brothers, and C. Mondavi & Sons (Charles Krug). The sign is not big enough to list the wineries now populating the valley.

Like Draper, Stewart, and the Mondavis, Frederick Hoyt McCrea came to St. Helena in 1943. An advertising executive, he too thought he'd give Mother Nature a run for her money. In 1948 he and Eleanor began planting their stony hillsides to Chardonnay and other varieties, finally bonding their Stony Hill winery in 1951.

In 1952 a young Hanns Kornell leased the former Tribuno Winery in Sonoma, a prelude to moving his operations to St. Helena six years later. Kornell then took over the old Larkmead Winery, formerly operated by the Salmina family.

Among the great winemakers in the valley in the fifties and sixties were a pair who toiled at wineries across the street from one another for better than sixty years between them. George Deuer presided over the cellars of Inglenook from Repeal until the middle sixties, while Andre Tchelistcheff held court at Beaulieu from 1938 through 1973. Together they defined Rutherford Cabernet Sauvignon for the world.

Jerome Draper Sr. points to the vast contrast between grape growing in the fifties and what it is today. "We didn't know as much then as we do today," says Draper. "When we were first planting Napa Gamay I told my foreman to pick out 'pretty vines.' Well, they happened to have leaf roll. We've learned a tremendous amount from Davis since that time. In the fifties we weren't always sure of being able to sell grapes. Today there's keen competition for quality grapes. Those of us in the hills have the opportunity to sell our grapes to small wineries for big premiums. We probably pay ten times as much for labor as we did then, but we're also paid at least ten times as much for the grapes."

The early sixties saw the revival of two winegrowing operations that are still going strong. Joe Heitz took over Leon Brendel's winery and gave it dimensions that Brendel couldn't possibly have imagined. Jack Davies left management consulting for large corporations to give new life to Jacob Schram's creation of a century before.

Through the forties and fifties the number of wineries in the valley hovered around forty. By 1966 that number had shrunk to twenty-six, of which fourteen were in and around St. Helena. Sixteen of those twenty-six are still in business.

Yet a firm foundation had been laid by generations of winegrowers. A wine boom was in the offing and the time pregnant for winemen of energy, enthusiasm, and optimism. In 1966 a man who exudes those qualities built the first new Napa Valley winery of any size since Repeal. His confidence spread, slowly at first, then with the rapidity of a rangeland fire.

The valley's northernmost vineyard.

The Modern Era

Nineteen sixty-six was a slow news year. The withdrawal of French troops from N A T O and the initiation of Medicare were the highlights. In the Napa Valley, on the other hand, things were in ferment.

The most significant expansion of winegrowing in the Napa Valley dates from that year. It is a clear point of demarcation. Three quarters of the Napa Valley wineries that crushed in 1978 have come into existence since Robert Mondavi built his Spanish-styled winery in Oakville. His vitality and optimism are symbolic of the new spirit of Napa Valley winegrowing.

Freemark Abbey was reorganized the following year and Bud van Loben Sels was putting Oakville Vineyards together. Mike Robbins founded Spring Mountain in the basement of a stately old Victorian in 1968, and 1969 saw the beginnings of Chappellet and Sterlin . Cuvaison and Yverdon came into being with the frosts of 1970, then there was a lull for a year. It was the lull before the storm.

Eleven new wineries were bonded in the rains of 1972, and eight more in the warm season of '73. The following years saw three, five, and two additional bonds before things began heating up again. Seven wineries crushed for the first time in 1977 and ten opened their doors in 1978. It's been like the old baseball cliche: You can't tell the players without a program.

It's also exciting. There's a vitality here that the valley hasn't seen since the innocent days prior to Prohibition and phylloxera. It is, fortunately, a vitality whose foundation is replete with hard work and sound practices.

Not that the road to success has been paved with yellow bricks or blocks of gold. There will always be casualties in a business that requires inspiration as well as capital. Some wineries, like Cuvaison and Franciscan, had shaky starts. Oakville, Pillsbury (Souverain), and Lyncrest had shakier finishes.

Neither will many of the newest wineries challenge anybody in volume. Only Rutherford Hill and Round Hill of the new wineries of the last five years are doing anywhere near 30,000 cases a year. Most of the new entries are small to tiny operations whose owner/operators are looking for quality in a limited number of wines.

Even assuming that per capita wine consumption continues to increase in only modest increments, there will clearly be a need for far more wine than even dozens of small new wineries can produce. American per capita consumption is now pegged at about two gallons per person per year, about four times what it was forty years ago.

Winemakers everywhere feel the lure of the Napa Valley. Tiny ZD Winery is moving its operation to the Silverado Trail east of Rutherford. Al Baxter is planning to move his Veedercrest to the hills of Mt. Veeder. Several other winery owners have visions of moving their operations to the magical valley once their labels are more firmly embraced by the consumer.

The Napa Valley has long been found alluring by visitors as well. In 1889 the trip from San Francisco to the Napa Valley wineries was advertised as an all day outing via Southern Pacific Railroad. Today well over a million visitors make the northward trek up Highway 29 each year, and the greater number of them stop to freely tour and taste at a winery or two.

Early in 1978 there was, for a short time, talk of charging visitors for wine tasting (as Sterling has done). Though the concept was quickly discarded, it must be noted that most of the smaller wineries have neither the wine nor the time to give to visitors. Such wineries list their hours as "by appointment only," and hope that their fans will respect that request.

Most visitors come to the valley from the Bay Area. Driving north from Napa, the most direct route is State Highway 29, "The Wine Road."

Even from Napa the incredible hulk of Mt. St. Helena can be seen at the far end of the vine-cloaked valley. It is difficult to appreciate the density of vine-lands except by flying over the valley in late spring, when the greatest part of the valley floor is lush with greenery that is almost entirely grape vine.

It is easy to while away whole days at a time while exploring, at a leisurely pace, the valley's many attractions. "Hurry" is not in the local vocabulary, save on October mornings when rain clouds threaten.

Yountville offers the splendid diversity of Vintage 1870, a tantalizing shopping complex built around an old brick winery. Across the highway is Domaine Chandon, with its fabulous French restaurant. The valley widens spectacularly north of Yountville, only to close again as St. Helena is approached, as if nar-

Oakville is little more than a whistle stop but for the excellent tours offered by the Robert Mondavi Winery.

Rutherford had only three wineries in 1966; today there are fourteen with Rutherford addresses. Those with seniority are Beaulieu and Inglenook, the one with its new visitor center and theatre, the other with its cool stone cellars and the ghost of Captain Niebaum lurking about.

St. Helena is still center ring. Twenty-two wineries claim a St. Helena address, but the most popular attractions continue to be the celebrated Rhine House of the Beringers and the hulking presence of Greystone Cellars, now the sparkling wine facility of the Christian Brothers. They stand at each end of the "archway of elms," planted by Frederick and Jacob Beringer in the mid-1880 s.

In 1978 the city of St. Helena enclosed 2900 acres. Of that, nearly half (1400) were in vineyards, protected by the general plan. The Christian Brothers had 130, Beringer 115, and Charles Krug 100 acres. Even the high school had 11 acres of vines.

Several enchanting hours might be spent browsing through the new quarters of the Napa Valley Wine Library at the new St. Helena Public Library, dedicated in 1979. The Napa Valley Wine Library Association, formally organized in 1963, performs several adjunct functions to the local wine industry. The Association's library now numbers better than 1200 volumes, plus over fifty taped interviews with veteran wine people. In addition to promoting the industry and protecting rowing its focus upon Mt. St. Helena at the head of the valley.

Manicured vineyards along the West Slope.

its past, the Association also plays the role of educator. Its summer wine appreciation courses are always booked well in advance and nearly five hundred people now attend each year.

Approaching Calistoga, that gleaming white "monastery" on the hill is Sterling Vineyards, reached by an aerial tramway. The self-guided tour is particularly instructive.

Before swinging back down the valley along the Silverado Trail (the route of fortune hunters seeking silver in another century), appropriate side trips would include Spring Mountain, where grapes of intense flavors are grown, and Pope Valley to the east, a secluded enclave where a single winery competes only with a sky diving ranch for attention.

Napa Valley's winegrowing industry has experienced ebb and flow many times through its lively history. There is little question but that its flow is full today and may be fuller still tomorrow. The Valley's prestige was enhanced by the strong showing of its wines at the touted Paris tasting of 1976, and 1979 has seen Napa Valley wines being exported to France.

The continued expansion of winegrowing in the Napa Valley adds vitality to an already vital industry and further insures its stability and success. It was Robert Louis Stevenson, in *El Dorado*, who said, "To travel hopefully is a better thing than to arrive, and the true success is to labour." Those who grow wine in the Napa Valley have long been hopeful travelers who know the values of honest, uplifting labor.

California

Oregon

Nevada

Pacific Ocean

Arizona

Mexico

Napa Valley

South

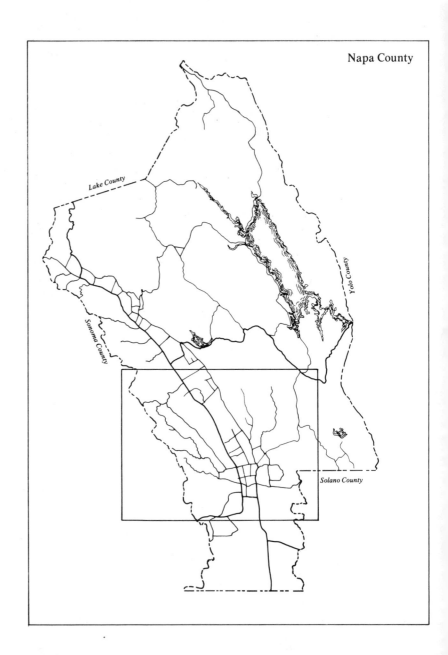

Napa County

Lake County

Sonoma County

Yolo County

Solano County

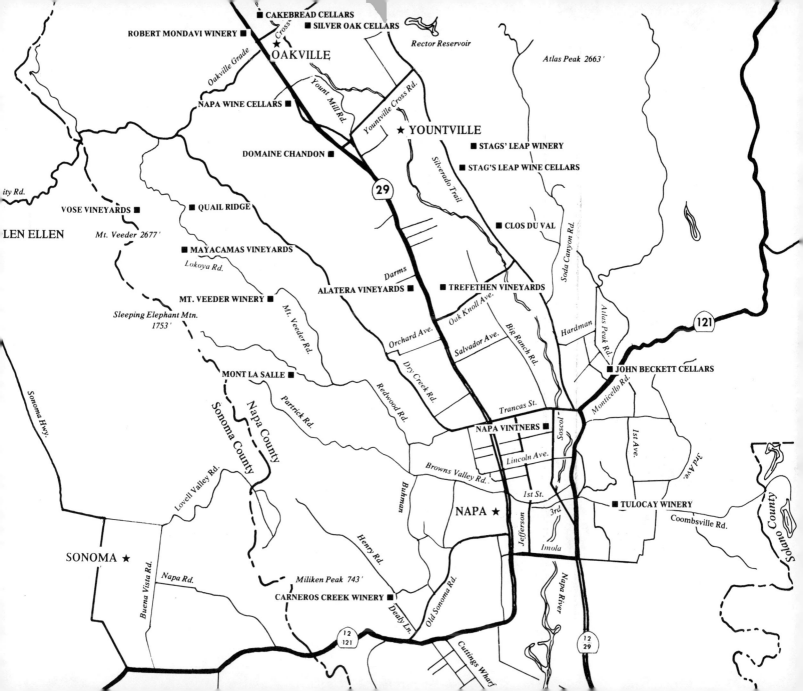

California

Oregon

Nevada

Pacific Ocean

Arizona

Mexico

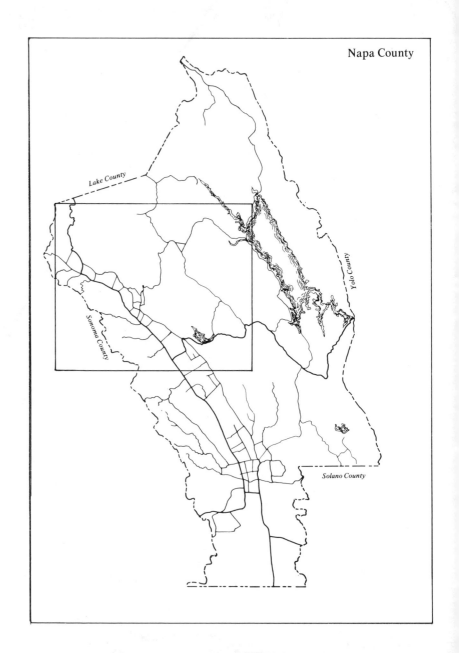

Napa County

Lake County

Sonoma County

Yolo County

Solano County

Napa Valley
North

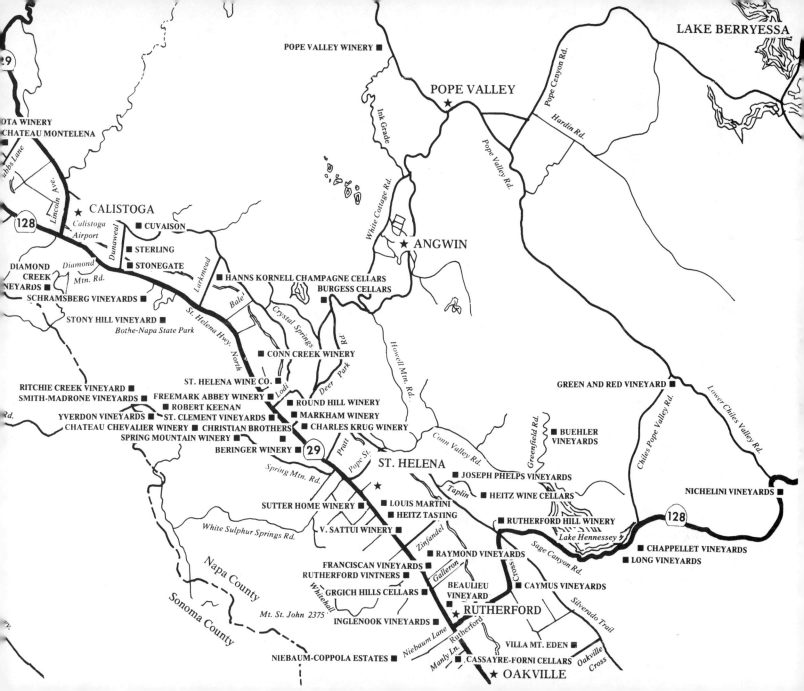

Chardonnay grape cluster

The Wineries

Carneros Creek Winery

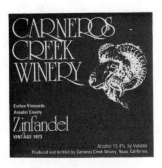

At the foot of Milliken Peak is Carneros Creek Winery, the southernmost winery of the Napa Valley. *Carnero*, in Spanish, refers to a male sheep. Indeed, the Carneros district was once home to hordes of the woolly beasts. But now grape vines populate much of the cool district.

Carneros Creek has made a name for itself with its sturdy, thick Zinfandels and Cabernets from Amador County's Esola and Eschen Vineyards. Thus the stout ram's head on its label may be considered doubly appropriate. However the ultimate goal of partner/winemaker Francis Mahoney is to produce elegant Carneros Pinot Noirs and Chardonnays, with character akin to the French Burgundies he is so fond of.

Mahoney feels that the climate of the Carneros is vital, particularly with Pinot Noir. "The fog sits on the vineyards in the mornings during the summer," he says, "usually burning off by around ten. The afternoons are warm, but cool off rapidly when the evening winds come in off the San Pablo Bay. With the cooler weather, we get better acid out here, hence a more balanced must."

Carneros Creek Winery began its evolution in 1971 when Balfour and Anita Gibson, owners of Connoisseur Wine Imports in San Francisco, needed to make some wine to maintain a winery license that had come with the store. (Interestingly, Anita Gibson is the great granddaughter of Elias J. "Lucky" Baldwin, who produced medal-winning wines from the 1200 acre vineyard at his famous Santa Anita Ranch in Southern California.) Their first wine was actually made at the Bryant Street store in the city in 1972.

The winery was constructed next to Carneros Creek in 1973 and expanded in 1978. Two banks of stainless steel fermenters stand under a projected roof behind the winery. Pinot Noirs are fermented in the two open topped fermenters so that the hard cap can be punched down—literally, kicked down—before pumping over is done to increase extraction. Usually about half of the stems are added back to the bubbling Pinot Noir must.

Mahoney's interest in Carneros-grown Pinot Noir runs so deep that the winery, in conjunction with U.C. Davis, is running a clonal selection trial behind the winery. Three acres there are planted to 20 different clones of Pinot Noir. Each is planted in three soil zones: rock with sandy loam, deep alluvial sandy loam, and gravel.

Carneros Creek Winery added Sauvignon Blanc to its production in 1979. Says Mahoney, "I like Sauvignon Blanc as a wine. It is easily made and it doesn't require a lot of new cooperage or fancy equipment, like a centrifuge." He also dabbles with other varieties on occasion, having produced small lots of Ruby Cabernet, Petite Sirah, and White Riesling.

Mount Veeder Winery

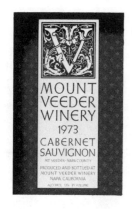

Mike Bernstein left his San Francisco practice of consumer protection and antitrust law in April of 1971 to take a year's leave of absence. He wanted to see if he could handle farming. For a living.

Eight years earlier Bernstein had answered an ad in the *Wall Street Journal* for a summer home set among the hills and valleys on Mt. Veeder, an extinct volcano north and west of Napa. What he found were two rickety houses, an orchard of French prunes and Satsuma plums, plus a variety of other fruit bearing trees.

That year Mike and his wife Arlene planted 60 grape vines: Mike dug the holes and Arlene planted the vines. They didn't know what variety they had and were elated when 57 of them prospered. (It turned out that they had two varieties: Grey Riesling and Cabernet. The Rieslings were grafted over to Cabernet.)

Mike says that he hadn't initially intended on becoming a farmer. He just started pruning the trees and vines a bit. Then he bought a chain saw, later a tractor. Each year he and Arlene planted a few more vines, watering them by hand. Before they knew it they had a few acres and Mike no longer had any inclination to return to the city. During one period, to keep bread on the table and flexibility in their schedules, the Bernsteins shared a four day a week public relations job at the Robert Mondavi Winery.

In 1973 they built their own winery on the site of the lower house. Kim Giles, an early partner in Mt. Veeder, played an important role in designing the efficient, three level, 20,000 gallon winery. The first two wines made were a Cabernet and a Zinfandel.

Bernstein will tell you that he's a winegrower, emphasizing the importance of the distinction. "Good wines are made by the winemaker, but fine wines are grown in the vineyard," he maintains. As a winegrower, Mike takes Cabernet Sauvignon most seriously. Early on he sought cuttings of all the Bordeaux varieties. Now, in addition to 13 acres of Cabernet Sauvignon, Mike's vineyards also boast 3 acres planted to Petite Verdot, Cabernet Franc, Malbec, and Merlot. "I probably have the largest planting of Petite Verdot outside of France," he says half seriously. (There are also 2 acres each of Zinfandel and Chenin Blanc.)

Indeed, eighty-five percent of Mt. Veeder's production is devoted to mouth-filling Cabernets, which are aged in French oak. All of Mike's wines are huge. To date, not one has weighed in at less than 13% alcohol.

A farmer first, Bernstein points to the importance of climate and soil for gaining the maturity he obviously coaxes from his grapes. His vineyard sites mostly face northeast, so they get the full benefit of morning sunlight without the intensity of afternoon heat. Even more important, in Mike's view, is the decomposed shale soil that provides thorough drainage. The soil is so porous that there is virtually no water table and they are forced, on occasion, to have drinking water trucked up to their mountain home.

Mayacamas Vineyards

Due to a fork in the range, the Mayacamas Mountains actually form both boundaries of the Napa Valley. The word itself comes from the Lokoya tribe, and means "the howl of the mountain lion." Indeed, cougars and bobcats are still heard and seen along the ridges and canyons of the range.

The stone winery building that houses the present Mayacamas winery was built in 1889 by John Henry Fisher, a sword engraver from Stuttgart. Fisher was a pickle canner in San Francisco when he founded the winery, which he called Mt. Veeder Vineyards. He produced bulk red and white table wines from Zinfandel and "Sweetwater" grapes and built a small distillery. Fisher's cannery was wiped out by the 1906 quake and his assets assigned to Owens-Illinois in lieu of his unpaid glass bill. The Pickle Canyon property, including the winery and vineyards, had many owners before coming to Jack and Mary Taylor in 1941.

The Taylors were amateurs possessed of great enthusiasm and endurance. Rabbits, deer, and birds of all description robbed them of vines and crop many times before they were able to successfully re-establish vineyards and winery, renamed Mayacamas. Through grit and determination they carved broad terraces out of the rocky, stubborn hillsides of the extinct volcano, planting the low yielding Wente clone of Chardonnay.

The Taylors turned the distillery into a cozy little home, incorporated and expanded the winery, and built a wine list of 17 different wines, including sparkling wines and three varietal roses. Many of these were sold under the secondary label, "Lokoya."

In 1968 they sold the business to a partnership headed by Bob and Noni Travers. A former investment banker, Travers eliminated the Lokoya label and began to restrict the number of wines produced. About three-quarters of his production is now devoted to the rich, well-bred wines made from the 32 acres of Chardonnay and 12 acres of Cabernet Sauvignon grown at the winery.

While Chardonnay and Cabernet define Mayacamas, like any craftsman, Bob tries his hand at other varieties. Zinfandel has long been a standby. In 1977, after a European trip, he produced both a red and a rose from Pinot Noir. "A trip to Burgundy is always an inspiration," he says brightly.

Bordeaux provided the push for experimental lots of botrytised Semillon and Sauvignon Blanc. "I like a higher level of Sauvignon Blanc in the blend than the French do," says Bob. "Our wine will probably be at least thirty to forty percent Sauvignon Blanc, perhaps more."

The Mayacamas label is distinguished by the stylized, heraldic block "M." A closer look reveals that the lions rampant are holding hands, a deft touch of romance from the Taylors. A folksy newsletter, started by Mary Taylor, has introduced the wines to the Mayacamas faithful more or less regularly for thirty years.

Trefethen Vineyards

In December of 1978 the Trefethen family received one of five awards made by the Upper Napa Valley Associates for "excellence in the preservation or restoration of historic structures which symbolize the lifestyle of the valley in the 19th century." The award was for their dedicated restoration to useful service of the former Eshcol Winery, the second oldest wooden winery in the valley.

The Oak Knoll area was first planted to vines by Joseph W. Osborn, who in 1856 won the Agricultural Society's $40 prize for the best improved farm in California. In 1886 Napa bankers James and George Goodman had the preeminent winery architect of the time, Hamden W. McIntyre, design a three story wooden winery. Built to last with incredibly stout beams, the walls and ceilings are lined with tongue-and-grooved redwood.

The Goodmans named their property Eshcol, for the biblical brook (Numbers 13:23) where the men of Moses "cut down from thence a branch with one cluster of grapes, and they bare it between two upon a staff."

In 1895 a curious fellow by the name of J. Clark Fawver leased the property, purchasing it five years later. A beer drinker, Fawver wouldn't have wine served in his home. He was a farmer, though, and dearly loved the earth. He took pride in his vineyard, had wine made from his grapes, and sold the wine off in bulk. During Prohibition he actually enlarged the winery, which was leased to Beringer for storage after Fawver's death in 1940.

The 600 acre property was purchased in 1968 by Gene Trefethen, the former president of Kaiser Industries. The vineyards were entrusted to the care of Tony Baldini, who instituted a program of replanting parcels of the old vineyard each year. A model vineyard today, it is planted primarily to Pinot Noir and Chardonnay. Other varieties include Cabernet Sauvignon, White Riesling, Gewurztraminer, Zinfandel, and Merlot. Their quality is such that grapes not used by the Trefethens have been in great demand by such wineries as Domaine Chandon, Schramsberg, Robert Mondavi, Clos Du Val, Joseph Phelps, and Cakebread Cellars.

With the handsome, pumpkin-colored winery building restored and the vineyard producing, the Trefethens turned their attention to winemaking. Gene's son John, who is responsible for general winery and vineyard operations, is ably assisted by winemaker David Whitehouse. Janet Trefethen, John's wife, is responsible for marketing the finished product.

Trefethen's first wines were made in 1973, when the winery was being shared with Domaine Chandon, who had no facility then. Chardonnay and White Riesling were the first wines made. They were released in 1976. Trefethen's first red was the 1974 Cabernet, released in April of 1978, and their Eshcol Red (Cabernet, Mondeuse, and Merlot) was introduced later that year. A generic white (Eshcol Ranch) and Pinot Noir are also being added to the Trefethen roster.

Beckett Cellars

FROM THE CELLARS OF JOHN BECKETT

Lake County
Fumé Blanc
A DRY SAUVIGNON BLANC
Alcohol 12% by Volume
Made and Bottled by Beckett Cellars, Rutherford, California

If you look closely at the label you will see a man who looks for all the world like Henry the Eighth. That's John Beckett, and in period garb he would indeed do justice to our imagined likeness of the vaunted poet-lover-king. The vine-covered stone cellar behind him is the former Estee Winery, completed in 1885. The walls are 26 inches thick and over 300 feet of sandstone tunnel forms an "L" back into the hillside, turning north to exit into a nearby garden.

The winery is on Atlas Peak Road, just east of Napa on the road to the town of Monticello, which now lies beneath the waters of Lake Berryessa. At Repeal the building became the Hedgeside Distillery, which it remained for twenty years. When the company went out of business, the two-story structure was purchased by Napa Drayage and Warehouse Company owner Dale Buller.

In 1975 the northern portion of the stalwart building, including the tunnel, was leased by Buller to former construction man John H. Beckett. A native of the Bay Area, Beckett joined his father's construction company after serving in the Army Air Corps during World War II, flying C-47s over France and Germany.

After forming his own construction firm in Oakland, he purchased a prune and pear ranch in Kelsey-ville, Lake County. In 1967, ten years after buying the ranch, he pulled the prunes and planted 110 acres to Cabernet Sauvignon. When the vines were mature, the grapes went to Robert Mondavi.

"I had always enjoyed drinking wine," says Beckett. "So when I got into the grape business it seemed a logical step to move on to winemaking. Since there were no crushing facilities in Lake County, I started looking around Napa County. When I found this place, I stopped looking."

Beckett stores and ages his wines in the barrel-lined tunnel in the former distillery, but they are crushed, fermented, and bottled at Rutherford Hill Winery under the guidance of winemaker Phil Baxter. "I am very pleased to have found Phil," notes Beckett. "He has taught me a lot, and he and I like the same flavors. It's a good partnership."

Beckett's first three crushes were devoted to Cabernet Sauvignons possessing strong varietal character and maturing young. In 1978 he began crushing Sauvignon Blanc and Johannisberg Riesling from a former partner's 40 acre vineyard near Upper Lake (Lake County). He would have crushed Gewurztraminer as well, but the birds got to it before the pickers could.

The first Beckett Cellars wines came on the market in September 1978 and already Beckett can boast of international sales. Samples of his wines were taken to Germany by a friendly San Franciscan, who helped cut governmental red tape when the wines were well received there.

Clos du Val Vineyards

It should be no surprise that Bernard Portet's Cabernet Sauvignons and Zinfandels are, stylistically, Bordeaux wines. Bernard is, after all, the oldest son of Andre Portet, the former technical director at Chateau Lafite. A graduate of Montpellier University, with a degree in agronomy and engineering, Bernard had also had experience in practical winemaking before coming to California.

Portet was hired by an American Francophile who was interested in creating fine Bordeaux wines. The original plan was to purchase or build a small chateau in Bordeaux, but they found the costs exorbitant. So Portet embarked on a global mission to select the best location for growing Cabernet Sauvignon. "The Napa Valley and Australia both looked good, but we chose to come here first," says Portet.

Portet's ability was immediately evident when he produced one of California's finest Cabernets in 1972, which was an otherwise dismal year for the variety. That and the following year's harvests were carried out primarily at the old Occidental Winery, just north of Clos Du Val's permanent home. A three story stone structure, Occidental was built in 1878 by T.L. Grigsby, who had previously participated in Sonoma's Bear Flag Revolt.

Portet's wines both have great depth of character. His Zinfandels are by far the more substantial wines, in terms of body. "Zinfandel can handle more tannin than Cabernet can," notes the slender, curly-haired Portet. "Cabernet needs lower alcohol, so I try to make it rounder, more complex. Balanced without being terribly big."

Shortly after Clos Du Val was on the map, Portet headed back to Australia to start a sister company in the township of Moonambel, Victoria province. Called Taltarni Vineyards, it had its first commercial crush in 1977 under the direction of winemaker Dominique Portet, Bernard's brother. Since the seasons are reversed, Bernard is able to act as consultant at Taltarni each winter (summer there). [It's a winemaker's dream to have two vintage a year to work with.] "It is drier than Bordeaux in their summer," says Portet, "and colder in their winter. We think that Cabernet Sauvignon, Chardonnay, and Sauvignon Blanc will do particularly well there."

The Clos Du Val Winery is aesthetically austere, a functional facility with no pretentions of being a showplace. Visitors, in fact, are asked to make prior appointments. Set against the eastern foothills of the valley, it is nearly surrounded by the Chimney Rock Golf Course. Better than a hundred acres of Cabernet, Merlot, and Zinfandel extend northward from the winery's cypress and magnolia-lined driveway toward the rocky prominence of Stag's Leap.

Clos Du Val has a rarely used second label: "Granval." Cabernets with high varietal character were left unblended for the Granval label in 1975 and 1977. Earlier, a 1974 Zinfandel (of a lighter style than that usually employed by Bernard) was bottled under the then "Gran Val" label.

Stag's Leap Wine Cellars

Warren Winiarski came to winegrowing from an academic career. The former professor of political science at the University of Chicago began by serving a pair of two year apprenticeships, first with Lee Stewart at Souverain, then at the Robert Mondavi Winery in Oakville.

By 1970 he had put in a forty-four acre vineyard of Cabernet Sauvignon and Merlot at the foot of the jutting tor known as Stag's Leap. In 1972 winery construction was begun and the initial crush held at Oakville Vineyards. The winery, simple but efficient in design, stands in a grove of oaks along the Silverado Trail a mile north of Clos Du Val. A second building—which houses barrel and case goods storage, a lab, a kitchen, and the bottling line—was added five years later.

Stag's Leap gained quick prominence when the Cabernet from Warren's second vintage swept a classy field at the ballyhooed Paris Tasting of 1976.

Warren talks about his stylistic goals for the Stag's Leap Cabernet Sauvignons: "We are looking for wines of enormous depth," says Winiarski, "with great definition of varietal character and a gracious suppleness of fruit that is fleshy in texture. We are not, however, interested in making any twenty-five year wines as such. We're not interested in making museum pieces."

The Stag's Leap Cabernets and Merlots are both from the vineyard below the winery. Where the Cabernet is softened with Merlot, the Merlot is made more sturdy by the addition of Cabernet. The proportions differ with the vintage. Indeed, various blocs of the vineyard are harvested at different times so that appropriate ripeness is achieved in each instance.

Warren believes strongly that it is the minutiae that separates great wines from the merely good. "Every effort made to get down to minute considerations and care, both in the vineyard and in the winery, will show up in the long run. The coincidence, too, of economics and effort is there. When you spare no efforts, the result is a wine that lives up to its price. I'm sure that that is what makes this all so attractive to me."

The whole Winiarski family participates in the venture. Barbara Winiarski helped design the label, handles publicity, and is possessed of a finely-tuned palate. Children Catherine, Stephen, and Julia are often pressed into service at the winery.

In addition to Cabernet and Merlot, Stag's Leap produces Gamay Beaujolais, Johannisberg Riesling, and Chardonnay. The latter pair both come from the cool hills east of Napa—the Riesling from Birkmyer Vineyards, the Chardonnay from the Haynes Vineyard. In all wines, Warren looks for a balanced elegance. "I've never cared for excessive wood in a wine," Warren notes.

Stags' Leap Winery

Stags Leap Vineyard
Napa Valley
Chenin Blanc
1973

A split-level road directs you east off the Silverado Trail, past olive trees and vines, into a pocket valley. A straight, walnut-lined drive, flanked by vineyards, gives way to the hillside, palm trees, an old stone winery, and the former Stags' Leap Manor Hotel, now the home of Carl and Joanne Doumani.

The manor house had been completed in 1891 or so by Chicago financier Horace Chase, who is said to have bestowed the name Stags' Leap on the rocky promontory that stands guard over this secluded section of the Napa Valley. The three story structure was turned into a hotel in 1920 by its subsequent owner, Fred Grange. It quickly became a popular hangout for those who pretended that Prohibition did not exist and for whom "depression" had no economic meaning. The hotel remained open until 1953.

Carl Doumani had been a restaurateur in his native Los Angeles before he decided to show his four children a different way of life. So he and Joanne bought the 400 acre estate from Ed Reiss in 1970 and began the seemingly endless job of restoration. The wooden third story of the former hotel was removed and the lower two levels, made of cut stone, became the Doumani residence. A stained glass window with the Chase family coat of arms was restored to its place in a south window. Its motto, taken from Virgil, is the first half of the phrase, *Ne cede malis, sed contra audentior ito* (Yield not to misfortunes, but go more boldly to meet them).

The Doumanis have been required to heed that motto. The winery has been embroiled in a continuing legal battle over its very name with nearby Stag's Leap Wine Cellars. A further right-of-way hassle has delayed zoning discussions toward Carl's goal of opening a small, seven-room inn and restaurant.

Doumani has been yearly improving the 100 acre vineyard, which is planted primarily to Cabernet, Petite Sirah, and Chenin Blanc. The latter two represent the primary wines Doumani produced, having been made since 1972 at the Souverain/Rutherford Hill facility.

In the meantime Carl has been working to put the original winery into functional order. He has been aging his wines in the 120 foot tunnel that bores into the hillside from the back of the stone building that Chase had constructed around the turn of the century. The main building later burned. The stone walls remained, standing forlornly as a monument to past glories.

In the fall of 1978 Doumani poured a concrete pad for the interior floor, rebuilt the interior walls with redwood, and roofed the 50 by 60 foot structure. Two stained glass windows have been designed to shine in the ornate window spaces flanking the arched front doorway. One window represents spring in lush green and blue hues; the other shows autumn in warm shades of orange and brown.

Domaine Chandon

There was no one to ride horseback through the valley shouting, "The French are coming! The French are coming!" There was, nevertheless, a considerable stir among the winegrowing establishment at the 1973 announcement that a prestigious French Champagne company had purchased 1200 acres of prime vineland in Yountville, the Carneros, and on Mount Veeder.

The company was Moet-Hennessy, a Paris holding company made up of Moet & Chandon, Mercier, and Ruinart Champagnes, Hennessy Cognac, and Dior perfumes. They had several reasons for looking to California. First, they saw an escalating demand for sparkling wines in the world market. Second, the French district of Champagne, due to restrictive appellation of origin laws, has almost nonexistent growth potential. Third, their premier winemaker, Edmond Maudiere, had tasted a broad selection of Napa Valley wines and adjudged them suitable for the Moet style.

An experimental vintage was conducted in 1973 in rented space at Trefethen Vineyards winery, with Maudiere testing a dozen potential Napa Valley varieties, from Green Hungarian to Colombard. While there had been little doubt that Chardonnay and Pinot Noir would predominate in the blend of Chandon's primary offering, there was considerable room for the learning as to what other varieties might prove beneficial to the blend. Pinot Blanc turned out to be thoroughly compatible, so much so that nearly 200 acres at the Mount Veeder and Carneros ranches have since been planted to that variety.

Chandon's Napa Valley Brut (labeled "Sparkling Wine" and not Champagne) is the company's flagship and will eventually account for nearly three-quarters of the winery's production. Chandon's other sparkler is Blanc de Noirs, made entirely from Pinot Noir grapes that are brought directly from the vines to the press in order to minimize color extraction (which would be increased by crushing and stemming). Neither sparkling wine is vintage dated, as Maudiere follows the French practice of holding back 15 to 30% of the wines from each harvest, to be blended back into future cuvees for stylistic consistency.

Two table wines and one dessert wine are produced from the press wines. The Chardonnay and Pinot Noir Blanc are sold under the "Fred's Friends" label (whimsically named for Moet-Hennessy president Comte Frederic Chandon de Briailles) and the aperitif is dubbed "Panache."

Aside from its quality sparkling wines, Domaine Chandon stands apart for its stunningly attractive winery facility and its first-rate French restaurant. Adjacent to the Veterans Home, the restaurant, visitors center, and Champagne museum are open Wednesday through Sunday. You should know that there is a charge for tasting (which includes *hors d'oeuvres*) and that the restaurant, open for luncheon and dinner, has been so popular that reservations are essential.

Napa Wine Cellars

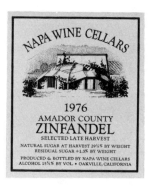

NAPA WINE CELLARS

1976
AMADOR COUNTY
ZINFANDEL
SELECTED LATE HARVEST
NATURAL SUGAR AT HARVEST 29½% BY WEIGHT
RESIDUAL SUGAR +1.3% BY WEIGHT
PRODUCED & BOTTLED BY NAPA WINE CELLARS
ALCOHOL 15½% BY VOL. • OAKVILLE, CALIFORNIA

"The winemaker may choose the style, but it's the vineyard that largely determines the wine," avers Charlie Woods. "I look for farmers who are proven professionals. It invariably ends up that the best have hillside grapes and low production."

Woods is the designer, builder, owner, and winemaker of Napa Wine Cellars. It is his feeling that, unless one has a very small operation, it is impossible to devote enough attention to both grape growing and winemaking. Considering the wines he has produced thus far, the philosophy suits Charlie just fine.

The dark-haired, soft-spoken Woods is a native of Great Falls, Montana. The son of a pharmacist, his maternal grandfather had been a bit of a winemaker in France. A University of Montana graduate, Charlie went into construction and engineering, building apartment complexes.

Not lacking for adventuresome spirit, he sold his business interests in 1972 and came to California with his wife Barbara. In Newport Beach they purchased a Columbia 43 and had ideas of sailing around the world. They went down to Mexico, then turned around and set a course for Seattle, where a friend of Charlie's had a marina. Winter storms closed in by the time they reached Monterey, so they struggled on into San Francisco to winter over. After visiting the Napa Valley on several occasions, Charlie sold the boat and purchased a piece of land a mile north of Yountville. It had three acres of Chardonnay and just enough room for the winery he had decided to build.

"I've always wanted to do a geodesic dome," he says. "It's an economical building, the technology is fascinating, and it represents the best possible use of space."

The low slung dome is the front half of the winery. A Dean Hopper stained glass window—of grape clusters and leaves in bright, natural colors—crowns the dome. Immediately below are five 1500 gallon Yugoslavian oak uprights, which hold Charlie's first year Cabernets. Small French oak barrels line the walls: Nevers for Cabernet's further aging, Limousin for Chardonnay, and American for Zinfandel.

The connected rear building is a 27 foot high truncated pyramid. Fermentation and bottling tanks line the front wall, oak barrels are stacked five high on one side, and case goods take up the remainder of the space. An extension is planned for the case goods.

The distinctively designed structure is just a half mile north of the Grape Vine Inn on Highway 29. Its buff colored walls are slowly being covered by Boston Ivy. Woods now opens his winery to visitors on weekends during the summer months, but hopes to be able to open it daily in the next year or so. Most of his efforts are directed toward Chardonnay, Cabernet, and Zinfandel, though he also dabbles in Gewurztraminer, White Riesling, and Pinot Noir.

Villa Mt. Eden

VILLA MT. EDEN

ESTABLISHED 1881

Estate *1976* Bottled
Napa Valley

Chardonnay

PRODUCED AND BOTTLED BY
VILLA MT. EDEN · OAKVILLE NAPA VALLEY, CALIFORNIA
ALCOHOL 12.0% BY VOLUME

The compound can be seen clearly from the Silverado Trail, nestled neatly in a small grove of trees north of the Oakville Cross Road, surrounded by open fields of grape vines. The clean white buildings, glistening in the sunlight, are trimmed in teal blue.

A greenish-blue, nearly turquoise, teal blue is a favorite of Anne Giannini McWilliams, who owns Villa Mt. Eden with her financier husband, James. The blue-green theme is carried through in many aspects of the winery/ranch operation. The soft color accents the Sebastian Titus drawing on the winery label; the boxed varietal name of each wine is likewise shaded in blue. Each bottle's lead foil capsule is a metallic shade of the color and Anne's upright piano in the office is a powder blue, ornately trimmed in white.

Given his credentials, one must presume that ranch manager and winemaker Nils Venge was not hired for his Danish blue eyes. Venge, whose father operates the wine importing firm of Venge & Co. in Los Angeles, turned down a track scholarship to U.C.L.A. to attend U.C. Davis. He took his degree in viticulture in 1967, having spent part of the previous crush working and learning at Heitz Cellars.

After a Viet Nam tour with the Navy, Nils was hired as viticulturist for the Charles Krug Winery by Peter Mondavi. In 1971 he left to share the job as vineyard manager at Sterling with Sloan Upton. While there he planted the hillside ranch at Petrified Forest Road, west of Calistoga.

A horse fancier, Anne McWilliams had been looking for a ranch in Pope Valley when Jim discovered the Mt. Eden Ranch. They purchased the 57 acre ranch from Constantine Ramsey in 1969, later adding an adjacent 30 acre parcel.

Initially the grapes were sold off to Allied and the Napa Valley Co-op. But three vintages of Gewurztraminer, vinified by Joe Heitz, indicated the quality of the vineyard. McWilliams hired Venge in February of 1973 to refurbish the vineyards, originally planted in 1881, and appoint the ancient buildings with stainless steel fermenters, French casks, and German ovals.

Eighty-three acres of the property are now planted to vines, primarily Cabernet Sauvignon and Chardonnay. The grapes are field crushed with a Mortl system, which allows better fruit retention in the Villa Mt. Eden Chardonnay, Chenin Blanc, and Gewurztraminer. They are cold fermented to dryness, usually over a period of nearly two months, as Venge prefers the Alsatian style.

A new garage, next to the office/lab, houses one of Anne's most prized possessions—her father's 1911 Hupmobile. An original ad, clothed in plastic, proclaims: "Exit the horse—enter the HUPMOBILE. 4 Cylinder, 20 H.P., $750." Dark blue, with black leather seats, the car is in mint condition. It was the first car owned by L.M. "Mario" Giannini, president of the Bank of America and son of its founder, A.P. Giannini.

Robert Mondavi Winery

The Robert Mondavi Winery is, at least stylistically, symbolic of the Spanish colonialism of early California. The structure is modestly set back from the highway amidst vines that will fill crushers and fermenters come the harvest. Designed by architect Cliff May, the Mission-like complex has a low profile, which is accentuated by the graceful curve of its central arch and its companion tower. Long covered corridors and Spanish tile floors complete the effect.

More importantly, the winery is symbolic of a spirit, a spirit that embodies vitality, strength, and enthusiasm. Those were necessary characteristics for a man who, at the age of 53, set out in 1966 to build the first new winery of any size in the Napa Valley since the end of Prohibition.

Thus, the winery is a touchstone for the Napa Valley and its founder an inspiration to those who work with him.

Robert Mondavi was one of four children born to Cesare and Rosa Mondavi in Virginia, Minnesota. While Robert and his brother, Peter, were still attending Stanford University, Cesare made a move that put a down payment on their future: he bought a Napa Valley winery. Though dessert wines were then king, Cesare knew that the future would be in table wines.

Robert joined his father at the old Sunny St. Helena Winery in 1937. Six years later the family sold their Acampo Winery and the Sunny St. Helena Winery so as to acquire the forelorn Charles Krug Winery. Even then Robert had an inquisitive mind that thrilled at daring new concepts. At Krug he was responsible for introducing a varietal Chenin Blanc with some residual sugar (1945). Nearly twenty years later he was among the first American producers to recognize the value of small European cooperage, this after a tour of European winegrowing regions.

That his investigative inclinations were often reined caused enough family friction that Robert eventually felt compelled to build his own launching pad.

It is a tribute to Robert Mondavi that his three children embrace fully his enthusiasm for the quest. Michael, the oldest, came to learn the business from the ground up, dragging hoses and cleaning fermentation tanks. He eventually became responsible for production, then sales and marketing. Since September of 1978 he has been the winery's president.

Daughter Marcia splits her time between the winery and her home in New York, where she is in charge of Eastern operations. Tim, a 1974 graduate of U.C. Davis, is in charge of wine production and oversees vineyard operations.

The winery itself is replete with innovative equipment. In 1969 Robert brought the first horizontal rotating tanks to the United States. Revolving at a steady three times a minute, the tanks allow maximum skin extraction during fermentation. This procedure gives great depth to the excellent Mondavi Cabernets.

The inner courtyard at Mondavi.

Sparkling stands of stainless steel fermenters are plugged into an I B M computer that monitors fermentation temperatures every eight minutes. Two centrifuges introduce a veritable forest of European and American oaks. Mondavi's full-time research man, Rich Arnold, has gotten to the point where he's testing different types of barrel stave chars.

After setting some pretty fair standards for Cabernet Sauvignon and Fume Blanc, the Mondavis are now investigating Pinot Noir with a vengeance. They have jury-rigged a device at the entrance of their crusher-stemmer that allows a portion of the stems to bypass the stemmer and go directly into the fermenters with the must. When the first Pinot Noir grapes come into the winery each season, experimental lots are made to determine the percentage of stem return that will be suitable for that vintage. The Mondavis also start the malolactic fermentation during the alcoholic fermentation to prevent potential off odors.

Mondavi's winery was initially built and operated in partnership with Fred Holmes and Ivan Schoch, and then with the Ranier Companies of Seattle. But after a January 1978 settlement whereby his interest in the Krug Winery was purchased by his brother and a sister, Bob Mondavi was eventually able, in August 1978, to obtain full ownership of his winery and vineyards.

In a 1977 settlement, the liquidation of Oakville Vineyards, Mondavi acquired the Oakville label, which will be used as a secondary label. Subsequently, Mondavi acquired the lease to the former Filice Winery at Acampo, where most of the Oakville wines and all of the Robert Mondavi Table Wines (generics) will be produced.

Though much attention is paid to things scientific in the winery, no little attention is paid to aesthetics. Mondavi personnel offer thorough tours and educational tastings in one of the several small tasting rooms in the south wing. The tasting and retail rooms house a succession of art exhibits throughout the year and the grassed, immaculate courtyard is the site of the celebrated Summer Jazz Concerts. One summer's lineup saw such greats as Dizzy Gillespie, Oscar Peterson, Roberta Flack, Benny Goodman, and Ella Fitzgerald. Most recently, gourmet cooking classes have been added, held in the well-equipped Vineyard Room.

Perhaps the most significant aspect of the Mondavi operation has been their ability to put forth remarkable quality from a winery that is by no means small. Much of that is a matter of attitude. Says Tim, "The fact that we have a large winery means that we can literally *play* with different, experimental concepts in the winery. We can try almost anything." Adds Marcia, "We've been fortunate enough to be able to grow without any loss of control, which has given us a wide range of choices. Thus, our style is the result of our choice." That, along with vitality, strength, and enthusiasm.

Cakebread Cellars

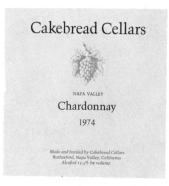

Cakebread Cellars

NAPA VALLEY

Chardonnay
1974

Made and bottled by Cakebread Cellars
Rutherford, Napa Valley, California
Alcohol 13.3% by volume

The small ad in the Oakland phone book proclaims, "Cakebread's Garage, Established 1927, Complete Automotive Service." Indeed, that is where Jack Cakebread spends most of his time, managing the business founded by his father, Lester, who had once grown almonds with Jack in Brentwood.

It was in 1972 that Jack and Dolores Cakebread bought the small ranch along the east side of St. Helena Highway, between Oakville and Rutherford. The land was mostly cow pasture and old vines before the Cakebreads ripped the soil and put in eighteen acres of Sauvignon Blanc, an acre and a half of Cabernet, and a half acre of Cabernet Franc.

Why Sauvignon Blanc? "We like to drink it," says their winemaker son, Bruce. "Dad had liked Robert Mondavi's Fume Blanc and we thought that people might appreciate a better selection in white wines. We seem to have guessed right."

Bruce Cakebread started his college days in San Luis Obispo at Cal Poly, where he majored in pomology (fruit science). "I like the outdoors," he says, "and I knew I wanted to go into agriculture." As Cakebread Cellars took on substance, he decided that winemaking would be it. So Bruce transferred to U.C. Davis, obtaining his degree in viticulture and enology in 1978.

Jack and Dolores had built a tiny barn in front of the one acre pond in 1972. They had their initial vintages crushed at the old Conradi Winery, high up on Spring Mountain (now Keenan Vineyards).

While Bruce was finishing his degree at Davis, the main winery building was completed. The interior walls are fir, the exterior redwood. Only fourteen feet wide, the long, narrow structure was designed to fit between vineyard and pond, so that no vines would have to be displaced. The eastern side of the winery is highly functional. Sliding doors—facing the deck where the crusher is placed—are of a configuration that they can be opened simultaneously during the crush.

In 1978 an old barn near the highway, complete with dirt floor and square nails, was refitted for additional barrel and case goods storage and a bottling line. Stainless steel fermenters stand guard behind the small structure.

The Cakebreads produce four wines: Sauvignon Blanc, Cabernet Sauvignon, Chardonnay, and Zinfandel. The Cabernet comes from the fine Stag's Leap vineyard of Dick Steltzner, Chardonnay grapes are purchased from Trefethen Vineyards, and Zinfandel is picked from 60 year old vines near Angwin.

Jack, in addition to auto repair and winemaking, counts photography high among his skills. He first started taking pictures while in Europe with the Air Force, and later free lanced as a professional. He has done N F L books and took most of the photographs illustrating Nathan Chroman's book, *The Treasury of American Wines.*

The winery offers no tastings, but visitors can see the premises upon advance notice. Cakebread wines are sold primarily through a mailing list.

Inglenook Vineyards

NAPA VALLEY
JOHANNISBERG RIESLING
*A dry white table wine with fresh, fruity flavor
and blossoming 1974 aroma of the
noble Johannisberg Riesling grape. Serve chilled.
Produced and Bottled by Inglenook Vineyards
Rutherford, California. Alcohol 12% by Volume.*

A hundred years ago Thomas Alva Edison finally came up with the first practical incandescent light bulb at his Menlo Park laboratory. Across the continent, a 35 year old Finnish sea captain was committing himself to the landlocked existence of a winegrower.

In January of 1979 Inglenook Vineyards celebrated the centennial of Captain Niebaum's legacy with a grand dinner at the Garden Court of San Francisco's Sheraton-Palace Hotel. The winery introduced its Centennial wine, the Estate Bottled 1974 Napa Valley Cask Cabernet Sauvignon, a huge, powerful wine that might well make the next centennial. Also served were superb Cabernets, Pinot Noirs, and Charbonos from the Inglenook library. As good as the heralded 1941 and 1943 Cabernets were, the 1959 Cabernet, grown in a warm, early year, proved the class of the evening. A round and sturdy wine, tannin still overshadowed its substantial fruit. At twenty years of age, it was nowhere near its peak.

Inglenook's creator was the meticulous Gustave Ferdinand Niebaum (originally Nybom). Born in Helsinki in 1842 (then under Russian domination), Niebaum took to the sea while in his teens. He had his own command at twenty-one and, before Lee's surrender at Appomattox Court House, had sailed to Russian America—Alaska.

Niebaum saw wonder and opportunity in the virgin territory. He bartered for furs and, when the U.S. acquired Alaska in 1867, he took a $600,000 shipload of furs into San Francisco Bay. He then helped form the Alaska Commercial Company, which specialized in the fur trade. In twenty years the company paid more in taxes to the American government than the U.S. had paid for the whole of "Seward's Folly."

After more than a decade of fur trading, Niebaum was ready to retire. It had been his ambition to build a ship to his own exacting specifications and sail the seas at his whim and leisure. There was but one problem: Mrs. Niebaum had not his love for salt air.

The Captain had made several trips to Europe while in the fur business, there acquiring a deep appreciation for the culture of the vine. When his chief aim was forestalled, he channeled his energies and fastidious nature into winegrowing. He carefully selected a thousand acre tract that drifted west from Rutherford up the slopes of Mount St. John. This he purchased in 1879 from W.C. Watson, who had given the property the name Inglenook (a Scottish term for a cozy fireside corner). Watson had probably chosen the name for the manner in which his home nestled into the valley's foothills.

Niebaum took his new task seriously. He read voraciously and had a standing order with a German bookseller to send him every publication on viticulture and enology printed in English, French, Italian, German, or Latin. Niebaum spoke five languages and read several others, and gradually accumulated a library of

Cask aging wines at Inglenook.

more than six hundred volumes on winegrowing.

Niebaum's monumental care showed both in the building he erected and the wines he fashioned therein. The Gothic stone and iron structure is a model of style and function. The winery was set into the hillside, its three levels providing the necessary flow pattern for grapes being transformed into wines, which rested finally in German white oak ovals on the pebbled ground floor.

The Captain was a forceful man who stood six foot two. He wore a long, flowing beard and was fond of surprise inspection tours, which he conducted wearing white gloves. Since the crushers, presses, tanks, and floors were to be scrubbed with soda and steamed every night, Niebaum expected to have unsoiled gloves at the conclusion of his tours.

Niebaum took great pains to protect his reputation, placing his seal and a wire closure on bottled wines in order to prevent counterfeiting. Said Frona Eunice Wait in 1889, "The reputation of Inglenook wines amply prove that, with perfect cultivation, a thorough knowledge of the soils, and the most rigid cleanliness in the vineyard and cellars good and drinkable wines can be produced in this State."

When Niebaum died in 1908, his widow Suzanne entrusted the winery's operations to her niece's husband, John Daniel Sr. Closed for the duration of Prohibition, Inglenook was reopened at Repeal under the guidance of Carl Bundschu of Sonoma. Mrs. Niebaum died in 1936, the winery going to John Daniel Jr. and his sister. Leon Adams says that Daniel upheld the Captain's motto of "Quality and not quantity" to the point of rarely, if ever, turning a profit. From 1935 to 1963 Inglenook wines were skillfully rendered by winemaker George Deuer. His best reds may outlive us all.

In 1964 Daniel sold Inglenook to Allied Grape Growers which, as United Vintners, later became part of Heublein.

Thomas A. Ferrell has been in charge of winemaking at Inglenook since 1971. A serious but sociable person, the curly-haired Ferrell has been working hard to maintain the Niebaum traditions. The Cabernet Sauvignon of 1975, for example, did not measure up to the standards set by Ferrell for Inglenook's "Cask" designation. So, for the first time, there was no Cask Cabernet that year.

There are three classes of Inglenook wines today. The top of the line are the Estate Bottled wines, produced solely from Napa Valley grapes. The vintage line comes from the northern coastal counties and the Navalle wines bear a California appellation. (Navalle is the name of a creek on the estate.) A line of ports and sherries also carries the Inglenook label.

In 1977 Ferrell produced three new wines for Inglenook: a delightfully fragrant Muscat Blanc, a Blanc de Noir from Gamay Beaujolais, and a Pinot Blanc—a dry, crisp Chenin Blanc.

Beaulieu Vineyards

The Napa Valley had a well-established reputation by the time a short, stocky French chemist purchased 120 acres of orchards and wheat fields just north of the Niebaum place in 1899. The man was Georges de Latour, and his legacy would include some of the most memorable Cabernet Sauvignons ever made in California.

He was born in Bordeaux in 1856 and studied chemistry at the Ecole Centrale in Paris. He came to San Francisco in 1883, the year the Brooklyn Bridge was opened and the same year the Wentes and Concannons became winegrowing neighbors in Livermore. He first put his chemistry to work in the gold mines of Tuolumne County. In 1888 he began the manufacture of baking powder from cream of tartar, and so came into contact with the wine business. He toured the wineries to obtain argols (the crude form of tartar that forms as a crush or deposit in wine tanks) and eventually established factories in the wine centers of Healdsburg, San Jose, Fresno, and Rutherford.

When he acquired the Rutherford property his wife christened it "Beaulieu," the beautiful place. Georges and Fernande loved beauty. They became patrons of the arts, maintained flowered formal gardens, and were widely renowned as providers of "lavish but sincere hospitality." President Herbert Hoover, Sir Winston Churchill, and visiting European nobles were guests at their San Francisco and Rutherford homes. The de Latours also made annual visits to France. On one, in 1924, their daughter Helene married winegrower Marquis Galcerand de Pins.

The winery, founded just after the turn of the century, produced notable wines from the beginning. In 1915 de Latour bought the Seneca Ewer Winery across from his home. Later enlarged, it remains the central core of Beaulieu today.

Curiously, the winery was put on financially solid footing during wine's darkest hour in America—Prohibition. Through the respect and friendship of San Francisco's Archbishop Patrick Riordan, de Latour kept the winery open as a supplier of altar wines. Additionally, by Prohibition's demise he had on hand a stock of well-aged table wines that rushed Beaulieu to the front during the confusion—replete with poorly made wines—of post-Prohibition winemaking. Reported Ernie Pyle in 1939, "Wine in the making is something alive and human to Georges de Latour. It is as human as a member of his family and must be treated as such. Winemaking is an art and a noble career."

The doughty Frenchman secured the future of Beaulieu in 1937 when he journeyed to France with his son-in-law to select a successor to retiring enologist Leon Bonnet. At the Institut National Agronomique in Paris Professor Paul Marsais recommended a Russian research enologist. Andre Tchelistcheff began his career at Beaulieu the following September, a career that would last over forty years and make him the most widely revered winemaker in America.

Georges de Latour died in 1940. He was accorded,

Vineyards seen from Beaulieu Champagne Cellars.

says Leon Adams, "the greatest funeral held in San Francisco in that decade, at which four archbishops presided." Fernande operated the winery until her death in 1951, when the estate went to her daughter. In 1969 Helene sold the winery and four of the BV vineyards to Heublein. She retained the original estate, with its sunken formal gardens, and the Cabernet Sauvignon vineyard (BV No. 1) that continues to produce BV's Private Reserve Cabernets. The original winery, across the street from the main winery, is leased to Heublein for the production of sparkling wines.

The impetus for champagnes came from Aldo Fabbrini, BV's eastern sales manager and brother of winery manager Nino Fabbrini. Nino brought Dr. Cosmo Ligorio (a chemistry professor at Long Island University who had been Beaulieu's technical representative in the east) west to develop standards for the BV Champagnes, which came on the market in 1955.

Still, Cabernet Sauvignon is the heart and soul of Beaulieu. That that is so is the direct result of Tchelistcheff's phenomenal success with Cabernets made from grapes grown in what he calls "the Rutherford dust." Though he could not convince de Latour to limit his production to Cabernet alone (or at most one or two other wines), he did obtain a separate cellar where the wine could be aged two years in American oak and two years in the bottle prior to release.

The year of de Latour's death saw the release of BV's first Georges de Latour Private Reserve Cabernet.

From the 1936 vintage, it sold for $1.50 per bottle. Today the current Private Reserves go for $10 and older vintages command upwards of $30 the bottle. It is no accident that well over half of BV's vineyards are planted to Cabernet in the Rutherford and Oakville area and that nearly half of the winery's production is of that varietal.

Winery president Legh F. Knowles Jr., a professional trumpeter in the swing era, believes that BV wines exhibit a distinctive personality. "Our wines are both rich and soft," says Knowles, "and those characteristics cause our wines to be drinkable at their release date."

Knowles, who has been with BV since 1962, also suggests that the production of quality wines is a team effort. The luminescence of Tchelistcheff notwithstanding, Beaulieu has always been blessed with many fine enologists. J.J. Ponti, who had joined de Latour in 1907, remained BV's winemaker until 1953. Through Tchelistcheff's reign, Andre was supported by such greats as Theo Rosenbrand (for over twenty years, now at Sterling) and Dick Peterson (The Monterey Vineyard). It was Andre's son, Dimitri, who interviewed Andre, Theo, and Dick to develop Beaulieu's 150 page Cellar Practices Manual.

Dimitri Tchelistcheff, BV's technical director for nearly a decade, provides the continuity for today's winemaking team. Tom Selfridge is winemaker, the enologist is Anthony Bell, and Mirjam Van Gelderen the chemist.

Caymus Vineyards

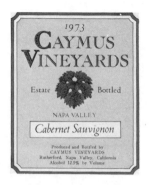

The importance of competent grape growing to fine wine is clearly exhibited in the operation of Caymus Vineyards. Owner Charles Wagner had been a grape grower for decades before becoming a winemaker as well. He was astute enough to alter his viticultural practices to meet the needs of winemaking. The primary change was a simple one, according to Wagner: control of production.

"Grape growers have historically believed that good sugar and acid were enough to make a great wine. That's not true. It is by limiting your crop, by concentrating the essence of the grape's flavors that great wines are made."

That concentration is clearly demonstrated by the Caymus wines. Wagner's *Oeil de Perdrix* (white Pinot Noir) has a deep bronze color and is long on texture and fruit. His red Pinot Noirs smell of freshly crushed mint and are rich and silky on the palate. The Caymus Zinfandels are round and pepperish, the Cabernet Sauvignons inky black and huge in the mouth.

Wagner has lived in Rutherford all his life. His father (also Charles) had come to the U.S. in 1885 from German Alsace, homesteaded in Nebraska, then worked in the brewing business in San Francisco. In 1906 he moved to Rutherford, where Charles was born six years later. The family made a little wine, which was bulked out.

Charles acquired Caymus Vineyards, just east of Rutherford on Conn Creek, in 1941. He purchased the plot from Minnie Freyermuth, the daughter of Henry H. Harris. Harris, who had purchased a part of the Caymus Rancho from George C. Yount, was a winegrower in the late 1800's. His stone winery, later remodeled into a fine mansion, still stands a few hundred yards north of Caymus Vineyards.

When Charles and Lorna Wagner bought the property it was planted entirely to prunes and walnuts. He pulled the walnuts first, later the prunes. He initially planted Burger grapes, a coarse variety that yields up to 16 tons an acre, but has since replanted most of the vineyard to prime varieties.

The winery was started in 1972. "We started with a very nominal investment, forty thousand dollars," says Wagner. "Today you'd have to have a half million to start."

Randy Dunn, a Davis-trained enologist, presides over a winery that is utilitarian to the point of being spartan. Stainless steel fermenters stand out of doors and the winery buildings are little more than insulated metal sheds crammed with Limousin oak.

Wagner's son, Chuck, has been a working partner at Caymus since his graduation from high school. The largest part of Caymus wines come from the 70 acres of well-tended vines surrounding the winery. But Charles, Chuck, and Randy have gone many places in search of fine Zinfandel, from Lake and Amador counties to Paso Robles and the Napa Valley. Half of the winery's production is devoted to red and white Pinot Noirs, all from estate grown grapes.

Rutherford Hill Winery

Rutherford Hill is the logical outgrowth of Freemark Abbey, a winery based upon vineyard-owning partners. As new vineyards came into production a difficult decision had to be made: Increase the production of Freemark Abbey or build a second winery?

Wisely, the latter choice was made. Fortunately, the former Souverain of Rutherford winery, owned by the faltering Pillsbury, became available at the time. Plans for a new winery (expensive) were gladly scrapped for the purchase of the thoroughly modern, albeit large, used winery (not so expensive).

It was an exceptional opportunity, for the massive, barn-like concrete structure, sheathed in cedar (built in 1972 from a John Marsh Davis design), had been outfitted with automated crushing and fermenting equipment, a sterile bottling room, and a vast barrel cellar stuffed with all sizes of American and European oak. The best part was that Phil Baxter, Souverain's experienced, Fresno State educated winemaker, agreed to stay on.

A new and larger partnership, with Freemark partners as the nucleus, purchased the facility in 1976 and renamed it Rutherford Hill Winery. The winery is capable of a 110,000 case production. That figure has, in fact, been achieved, but about half of the wines made are those custom crushed for several other wineries. It is an efficient use of the building's capabilities.

Managing partners Chuck Carpy and Bill Jaeger make it clear that Rutherford Hill is not a secondary label for Freemark Abbey. "Though the wines from both wineries will be marketed and sold by the same people, what few varietals are made by both wineries will be made differently by each," says Jaeger.

Chardonnay, for example, will be aged in Limousin oak; the Freemark Chardonnays are aged in Nevers. Rutherford Hill's Johannisberg Riesling is made with about one percent residual sugar, while Freemark's are often botrytised wines with high residual sugars. The Rutherford Hill Cabernet is blended with a higher percentage of Merlot than Freemark's.

The partners feel that Zinfandel may one day become the standard-bearer for Rutherford Hill. The grapes that Baxter vinifies come from 40 year old vines at the 1800 foot Atlas Peak vineyard of Giles Mead, who is the curator of the Los Angeles County Museum of Natural History. The wines bear the "Mead Ranch" appellation. Aged in Yugoslavian uprights and American oak barrels, they are cherry red in color, pungent with the smells of raspberry, and have a pepperish finish.

Rutherford Hill also produces a spicy, perfumed Gewurztraminer, Pinot Noir (aged in French oak), Pinot Noir Blanc, and Merlot.

The winery is only open to visitors on the second Saturday of each month. Tasting, tours, and sales are offered then from ten until four.

Chappellet Vineyards

Double letters abound in the names Donn and Molly Chappellet, but their winery is best understood in terms of threes. The winery's symbol is an equilateral triangle formed by three isosceles triangles. It represents the winery itself, a magnificent edifice of concrete, steel, and warm wood that was three years in the building.

Designed by an artist friend and engineered by Richard Keith, the pyramidal structure has three wings radiating out equally from the central work area. The rust colored metal roofs practically flow into the surrounding hillside of identically colored, iron-rich soil.

A burly, full-bearded man, Donn Chappellet looks every bit a mountain man, forging a new life out of the wild west. In a sense, he is. In 1967 he resolved to forsake the food vending company he and a partner had built into a multimillion dollar corporation. He couldn't go much further west from Beverly Hills, so Donn and Molly looked north to the Napa Valley.

The spot they found is near the peak of Pritchard Hill, overlooking Conn Valley and Lake Hennessey to the north. The winery is 1200 feet above sea level and the vineyards rise to the 1800 foot elevation.

Chappellet's first wine was a bone dry Chenin Blanc that immediately caught the fancy of wine lovers.

The following year, 1969, Chappellet had its first crush on Pritchard Hill, producing a Cabernet Sauvignon that people still talk about.

Chappellet puts a lot of effort into his Cabernets. Of the 95 acres of terraced vines planted in the red earth above his winery, nearly half of them are Cabernet. "We're looking for more finesse in California Cabernet," says winemaker Tony Soter. "We don't want the alcohol to inhibit the flavor, nor do we need the overripe flavors—like prunes—that are offensive in Cabernet. Mountain grapes are intense enough as it is."

The Chappellet Cabernets are fermented dry, then racked into 60 gallon Nevers oak for about two years. Blended with about 15% Merlot, they are comfortably under 13% alcohol. As such, they are rich, round wines of great depth.

The winery originally produced just Cabernet, Chenin Blanc, Chardonnay, and Johannisberg Riesling, but added Merlot when the crop was higher than usual in 1974. Generic wines are designated "Pritchard Hill Red" and "Pritchard Hill White." In 1977 Donn added Gamay to his roster, made from Napa Gamay grapes grown at Fritz Maytag's York Creek Vineyard on Spring Mountain. Aged a year in Nevers oak, Donn and Tony expect a full bodied wine that will age well.

Grapes are also purchased from three neighbors on Pritchard Hill. Their vineyards are farmed by Chappellet's own viticulturist Randy Mason, a Davis grad who has been with the winery since 1973.

Nichelini Vineyards

Nichelini
VINEYARD
PRIVATE RESERVE

NAPA VALLEY
ZINFANDEL

PRODUCED AND BOTTLED BY JAMES E. NICHELINI
BONDED WINERY NO. 843, ST. HELENA, CALIFORNIA
ALCOHOL 12½% BY VOLUME

A sturdy lime-green house, with white trim, is perched atop a stone cellar on the right side of Highway 128, nearly eleven miles east of Rutherford. With its accompanying wooden cellar, this is the comfortable, old-fashioned, roadside winery of James and Dorothy Nichelini. Literally roadside, for there is barely room to park between the red rust-coated hopper and crusher-stemmer and the blacktop of the state highway. A small stone tunnel stands opposite the winery.

The winery was built in 1890 by Nichelini's grandfather Anton, a native of Switzerland who had studied winemaking in France before coming to California to work in a large Sonoma Valley winery. In 1884 he homesteaded in Lower Chiles Valley, later building the winery from native stone, bonded with sand and lime. He could not afford cement.

Anton and Caterina Nichelini raised twelve children in the frame house above the winery. He planted a vineyard and sold his wines to the miners who mined magnesite nearby. When other wineries closed in 1919, Anton could not understand why he could not continue to earn an honest living. Only after a six month jail term (as a trustee) did he cease making wine.

Anton's son William took over the operation after the dreadful failure that was Prohibition. The Northern California sales representative for Beaulieu Vineyards, William Nichelini lived in Oakland and journeyed north on weekends to make enough wine each year to keep the license current. Each summer his son Jim would live with his grandmother, becoming more and more enamored of winegrowing.

In 1947, when the price of grapes dropped precipitously to $35 a ton, William pulled Jim out of high school to run the winery full time. By the mid-fifties Jim had introduced the Nichelini label and during the following decade he discarded first the gallon jug, then the half-gallon bottle. Now all Nichelini wines are sold in fifths.

"In the old days the old time Italian bachelors would come up here and we would fill their jugs and barrels," says Jim today. "We would sell it any way we could then. We were lucky if we could get rid of it. Now all the small wineries are short of wines, and it's just the beginning."

Jim produces his wines primarily from his own grapes, grown a half mile northwest of the winery. Loyal customers clamor for his specialities, Chenin Blanc and Sauvignon Vert, the latter a disappearing variety. He also grows and produces Petite Sirah, Cabernet, Zinfandel, and Gamay. In addition, Jim buys Carnelian from Winters and Semillon from nearby Pope Valley.

Jim used to entertain weekend visitors on his accordian, but plays only at private parties nowadays. Still, visitors will find a genial host and his touted open air terrace "tasting room." Jim's son, Jim Jr., lives in the frame house and may one day become the fourth generation of Nichelinis to operate the winery.

Grgich Hills Cellars

GRGICH HILLS

Napa Valley
JOHANNISBERG RIESLING
1977

PRODUCED AND BOTTLED BY GRGICH HILLS CELLAR
RUTHERFORD CALIFORNIA ALCOHOL 12.4% BY VOLUME

The vineyard owner and the winemaker joined forces in 1977. The former is Austin E. Hills of the San Francisco coffee family. He owns 140 acres of vines in Rutherford and east of Napa. The latter is Miljenko "Mike" Grgich, the Croatian-born winemaster who put Chateau Montelena on the map.

A patriot in his adopted country as well as his native, it was no coincidence that Mike chose the Fourth of July to break ground for the Grgich Hills winery. On that occasion he solemnly, and happily, blessed the earth with a bottle of 1973 Montelena Chardonnay (his Paris winner). For Grgich Hills is to be a Chardonnay house, where the wine will be of what Grgich calls "chateau quality."

The elfin, bright-eyed Grgich was born in Croatia (a fiercely independent part of Yugoslavia) in 1923, the youngest of eleven children. His family had both vineyard and winery, and Mike recalls helping tread grapes at age two. He took his degree in enology at the University of Zagreb, then came to the United States.

Grgich is particularly grateful for the direction he has received since coming to the Napa Valley in 1958. He worked first with Lee Stewart at Souverain. "Stewart gave me the impression that devotion and love for wine must exist to create fine wine," says Grgich. "That plus cleanliness."

After a brief stint at the Christian Brothers, Mike spent nine years at Beaulieu learning from Andre Tchelistcheff. "Andre brought the French influence to the Napa Valley," notes Grgich. "He accentuated the *art* of winemaking."

Art is important to Grgich as a means of achieving individuality. "Each wine that we make is and must be structurally different and distinctive," he avers. "When I first came to California I went to a winery to taste some of their wines. I sampled five white wines and they all tasted alike. There was no varietal character in any of them, there was nothing different about them."

After working at Beaulieu, Mike spent five years at Robert Mondavi (before going to Montelena). "Mondavi was a winery of action," says Mike. "There were so many experiments going on. There's no place in America like it for the learning."

Chardonnay is the stellar attraction at Grgich Hills. At least half the winery's production is devoted to the variety. What Mike looks for in Chardonnay is a medium bodied wine that retains delicacy and whose varietal character and oak marry into a unified bouquet.

About 30% of production will be Johannisberg Riesling, and the remainder Zinfandel. Cabernet Sauvignon will likely be added in a year or two. Mike looks for pure varietal aroma in his Rieslings and will produce botrytised wines only when the vintage demands it. Zinfandel, to Mike, is no ordinary wine. "It has a finesse, a delicacy that is special," he says with feeling. "Where you need a malolactic fermentation to soften Cabernet, it is not beneficial to Zinfandel. Zinfandel's natural berriness is tied to malic acid."

Rutherford Vintners

RUTHERFORD VINTNERS BRAND

CALIFORNIA 1974
Cabernet Sauvignon

Alcohol 12½% By Volume
Produced & Bottled By Napa Valley Cellars
St. Helena, Napa County, California

Bernard Louis Skoda may have gotten a late start in life, insofar as founding his own winery, but he's not the sort of person to waste time worrying about it. The vital, white haired sixty year old comes to his own venture with decades of experience in the wine trade and energy in abundance. "I feel ten years younger in getting my winery going," he says, and his broad smile shows it.

Skoda gained his early winemaking experience as a youth in his native French Alsace-Lorraine. The war in Europe saw him enlist in the French ski patrol. After the war he was an administrator for the United Nations Displaced Persons Bureau in Germany, where he met his helpmeet, Evelyn, who was a deputy director with the Canadian contingent.

Their work completed, the Skodas lived in Vancouver for six years, where their children — Louis and Jacqueline — were born. In 1954 they moved to Burbank, where Skoda was sales rep for Parrott & Co. Seven years later Louis Martini Sr. asked him to move north and join the Martini staff. Skoda was a mainstay at Martini for 15 years.

In 1967 the Skodas purchased a 25 acre plot a half mile north of the Rutherford Cross Road, planting it the following year to Cabernet Sauvignon. Later, with proceeds from their grape sales, they bought the current winery site and planted six acres of it to Johannis-berg Riesling. That was the easy job. Thinking winery all the while, they began the three month task of thinning the two acre jungle of eucalyptus that has been a valley landmark for over half a century.

In 1977 the reddish concrete block winery took shape, flanked by the eucalyptus grove, which is being landscaped on one side and preserved in its natural condition on the other. Inside, under 16 foot walls and a gracefully arched ceiling, stands a different sort of grove. Yugoslavian ovals line the north and south walls, American uprights form one aisle, and French and American barrels line the center. A lone, 2087 gallon German oval stands at the head of this grove, holding Skoda's Kabinett-styled Johannisberg Riesling.

Bernard and Evelyn Skoda pretty much run the winery themselves. Bernard makes the wines and does nearly all of his own selling, as befits a man who spent over 22 years in sales. Evelyn runs the office and retail-tasting room from the little house that sits just off of Highway 29. Their children put in many hours to assist in getting vineyards and winery established, but have now resumed careers in music (Jacqueline) and law (Louis).

Skoda produces his Cabernet, Riesling, and Pinot Noir (his primary output) from Napa Valley grapes, but looks to Fresno for his Muscat of Alexandria. The wine is highly aromatic and is fleshy and fruity on the palate, without being overly sweet. "Muscat is probably the most versatile of grapes," comments Skoda. "You can eat the grapes fresh, you can dry them for raisins, or you can make a thoroughly delightful wine." Skoda has done the latter.

Franciscan Vineyards

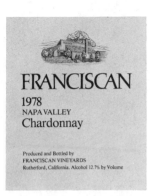

FRANCISCAN
1978
NAPA VALLEY
Chardonnay

Produced and Bottled by
FRANCISCAN VINEYARDS
Rutherford, California. Alcohol 12.7% by Volume

If Franciscan were a ship, one would be compelled to say that what exists today is a remarkable restoration of a double shipwreck. Four years ago there was nothing left but empty spars protruding from a lifeless, sandy beach. Today she's afloat with sails billowing.

If that sounds overly dramatic, you must remember that the winery was founded in the early years of this decade by a group of San Francisco investors who saw only stars. And red ink. They erected a magnificent redwood-faced edifice and, with their first crush in 1973, made nearly 300,000 gallons of wine. Nary a drop was sold before the venture had to be completely reorganized with the infusion of Canadian capital. The forty shareholders of the new group lasted scarcely a year before bankruptcy was declared.

The beached ship was taken over barely in time for the 1975 crush by Colorado developer Ray Duncan and veteran winemaker Justin Meyer. Together they charted a more realistic course. They started by selling off the uneven inventory at fire-sale prices, many of the wines going for a dollar a bottle under the now-defunct "Friar's Table" label.

Though Franciscan has never been connected with the church in any way, president and winemaker Justin Meyer was for 15 years a Christian Brother. Like his confreres, what he wanted most was to teach and coach youngsters, which he did for three years after his graduation from St. Mary's College. A stout, amiable sort, Justin looks like a winemaking monk. After his teaching stint he was assigned to the Christian Brothers' Mont La Salle winery, then sent to Davis to obtain his B.S. and M.S. in enology. In May, 1972, Justin left the order to become a consulting viticulturist/enologist.

As a winemaker Meyer is a firm believer in the quality of Oakville and Alexander Valley Cabernet Sauvignons. "We should learn from Bordeaux," he says. "They know what they do best, and they do it. Cabernet is what we do best here. The difficulty is that it's not very pragmatic to base over half your production on one wine. I'd like to, but it doesn't seem to fit into the American way of marketing. Yet."

Still, 62% of the 900 acres that Meyer and Duncan own in Oakville, Alexander Valley, and Lake County are planted to Cabernet Sauvignon and Merlot. (Indeed, a portion of their Alexander Valley grapes go to their Silver Oak Cellars, a winery which produces only unblended Cabernet Sauvignon.)

At Franciscan Meyer has consistently produced sound wines at decent prices. In 1975 he fermented the first commercial lot of Carnelian, which he made in the nouveau style. He is also proud of his Franciscan Burgundies, which have won successive golds in three L.A. County Fairs. The most recent, Cask 317, is a blend of Gamay, Petite Sirah, Pinot Noir, Cabernet Sauvignon, and Carnelian. It sells for less than $3 the fifth.

Raymond Vineyards

Roy Raymond Sr. had worked at Beringer for nearly forty years when the financial drain of inheritance taxes forced the sale of that historic winery to Nestle in 1970. (Four members of the second generation of Beringers had died within three years.) Raymond's wife, Mary Jane, is the daughter of Otto Beringer Sr. and the granddaughter of founder Jacob Beringer.

The Raymonds' two sons are both solid, husky young men. Roy Jr., who was in charge of Beringer's vineyards through the 1978 crush, has a business degree from U.C. Berkeley and later studied viticulture at the Davis campus. Winemaker Walter, who took his degree in business from Cal Poly (San Luis Obispo), later served his apprenticeship in the Beringer cellars.

The senior Raymond is a short, stocky, jovial man of great industry. "After we sold Beringer," he says, "we asked the boys what they wanted to do. They said, 'Let's put in a vineyard and winery of our own.' I told them, 'Fine, as long as I don't have to do any of the paperwork!'"

The closely-knit family purchased 90 acres at Zinfandel Lane and Wheeler Way. Roy Sr. and Roy Jr. already have their homes on the property and Walter is planning his. In 1971 they began planting 80 acres to vines—Cabernet Sauvignon, Chardonnay, Johannisberg Riesling, Chenin Blanc, Gamay, and Zinfandel.

Three years later they erected a temporary winery building, equipped it with ammonia-cooled Mueller fermenters and scads of small French oak, and began making wine.

They crushed just 50 tons that first year. Since then things have gone well enough that Walter has estimated their 1979 crush at ten times their initial endeavor.

The wines have been well received. Walter's 1975 botrytised Johannisberg Riesling earned a gold at the 1977 Los Angeles Fair and his 1976 Chardonnay was dubbed a "spectacular success." His Cabernets thus far have been uniformly soft and deep, even in their extreme youth.

Roy Jr. has all of the Raymond vines pruned on a cordon. The thinking behind that decision is that there is better exposure to air and sunlight, the vines are easier to prune and harvest (once the cordon is established), and that they can be easily machine harvested if need be. He uses a three wire vertical trellis to weave the canes through, which prevents the cordon from twisting under the weight of heavy fruit clusters.

The Raymonds began building their permanent winery toward the end of 1978. They hope to have the fermenting cellar finished before the 1979 crush and to complete the 20,000 square foot building shortly thereafter. The exterior will follow the design of Roy Raymond Senior's adjacent home: stonework at the base, with green inverted board-and-batting, and a shake roof. The Raymond "boys" are acting as their own contractors and are doing most of the work themselves.

Joseph Phelps Vineyards

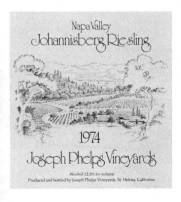

The old Spring Valley Schoolhouse provides the first impression. Dark green, neatly trimmed in white and topped by a belfry, it marks the turnoff from the Silverado Trail onto Taplin Road. A short distance brings one to the strikingly bold gateway, built with century old railroad bridge timbers. The horizontal trellis-work, a theme that is carried through in a winery breezeway, is supported by massive beams.

The winery itself, constructed of recycled redwood, features twin pavilions united by a mezzanine that houses offices and laboratory. The south wing shelters over 1300 French oak barrels, in gantries to the roof, and a new Seitz bottling line. The north wing, home to stainless steel fermenters, was recently added on to for a new press room. Around the corner, the cedar shingle roofline is being extended to form a more practical storage area for the winery's collection of large German ovals.

The integrity and charm of the physical plant is to the credit of owner Joseph Phelps, board chairman of Colorado's Hensel Phelps Construction Company. In California to fashion the two Souverain wineries in 1972, he purchased the nearby 670 acre Connolly Hereford Ranch. The following year he was joined by Geisenheim graduate Walter Schug, and vineyard and winery development commenced.

Schug has fully demonstrated his winemaking brilliance with several vintages and varieties of superb Johannisberg Riesling. In 1977 he added a golden, honey-thick late harvested, botrytised Gewurztraminer to his long list of credits. In conjunction with Phelps' interest, he is also exploring the California variations of French Syrah, the Rhone variety at the heart of the great Hermitage and Cote Rotie wines. Phelps' Syrah, which has improved with each vintage, is now displaying an expansive nose and cranberry-like fruit.

"We feel that Syrah will ultimately be at least the equivalent of Zinfandel in importance in California," says Phelps. "It may even rank with Cabernet and Pinot Noir as a classic variety. We've got twenty-one hillside acres planted to Syrah already and are putting in four more. One of our Calistoga growers will also put in Syrah, if he can get heat-treated budwood."

Phelps is so committed to developing Syrah that he is trying to obtain budwood of Viognier, a white variety grown in the upper Rhone Valley for blending with the wines of the Cote Rotie.

Each year the finest wine of the vintage receives the "Insignia" designation. The 1974 Phelps Insignia was a Napa Valley Cabernet Sauvignon. In 1975 the top of the line was the Merlot from John Stanton's Oakville vineyard (including 20% Cabernet) and the following year the nod went to Milt Eisle's Cabernet Sauvignon, grown in Calistoga. The 1977 Insignia wine is a blend of Cabernet, Cabernet Franc, and Merlot.

Heitz Wine Cellars

The understanding of Joe Heitz comes from two facets of the man: He is an educator and he possesses a keen, perceptive palate.

Joe is a seeker of quality. As such, he has little tolerance for imprecision, in himself or in others. As such, he has always been quick to share his knowledge and experience with others. His teaching abilities are highly praised by those who have served their winemaking apprenticeships under him. One winemaker, who now has his own winery, says, "Working with Joe was an invaluable experience. I got to do everything from cleaning filters and fixing pumps to operating the bottling line. One thing about Joe, he does things right."

Heitz became interested in wine while stationed in California with the Air Corps during World War II. While still in the service, he worked nights at the Italian Swiss Colony plant in nearby Clovis. Upon his discharge he enrolled at U.C. Davis, receiving his B.S. in 1949. During the next decade he worked at several wineries and taught at Fresno State. A judge at the California State Fair, he was also active in the Wine and Food Society.

In 1961 Joe and Alice Heitz purchased the tiny Leon Brendel Winery in St. Helena (next door to Louis Martini). Brendel's label was "Only One," a reference to the only wine he produced—Grignolino. To this day Joe carries on that tradition, producing both a red and a rose from Grignolino, each selling for less than $4.

In 1964 Joe and Alice bought the two story stone winery at the end of Taplin Road, which had been built by Anton Rossi in 1898. They planted 20 acres of the ranch to Grignolino and, in 1972, they completed a new winery and office complex adjacent to the stone winery and their home.

The key to the Heitz success is Joe's palate. As a winemaker, he knows that he can devote his attention to the production of just so many wines. So he purchases a number of wines, relying upon his critical judgment and blending ability to come up with good values. It is a reflection of his confidence in his ability that he labels such wines, "Perfected and Bottled By."

Joe's skill as a winemaker is constantly proven by his legendary "Martha's Vineyard" Cabernet Sauvignons. When he released the last of his classic 1969 vintage last year, the tab was $40 the fifth. At the same time, he acknowledged that the 1971 Martha's Vineyard had not met his expectations. So the wine was blended, designated Lot MZ-1, and offered at $7.50. Said Joe, "We certainly do not claim this is one of our great wines, but do believe it to be a sound value."

Heitz Cellars wines are sold through their tasting room (the former Brendel Winery) and by means of a newsletter written by Alice, who is also known for her culinary talents. Their oldest son David, a 1972 graduate of Fresno State, shares the winemaking responsibilities with Joe, and daughter Kathleen joined the staff in September, 1978.

V. Sattui Winery

1973
NAPA VALLEY
Dickerson Vineyards
Zinfandel
Cellared and Bottled By
V. Sattui Winery
ST. HELENA, CALIFORNIA
Alcohol 12% By Volume

Many of California's newest wineries are founded on the bedrock of a going vineyard operation. The sale of grapes provides the cash flow necessary to gradually expand the winery, until it becomes self-sustaining.

Daryl Sattui went about it a little differently when he brought the Sattui name back into California winemaking in 1975. Since Daryl had no vineyards, and wanted none, he put his entrepreneurial mind to work and came up with the St. Helena Cheese Factory.

"I wanted something that would, first of all, provide cash flow for the winery," says the tall, black-bearded, olive-eyed Sattui. "Secondly, I wanted something that would bring people into our winery, into our tasting room. I spent a year and a half investigating the possibilities and came up with a sixty page business plan."

Daryl had it down to the point that he knew he needed to be north of Oakville and south of Lodi Lane in order to appeal to hungry people. The answer: A cheese factory that features picnic tables in a walnut shaded park. The cheese factory is worth mention of its own merit, with over a hundred varieties of fresh cheese from all over the world, including Daryl's own smoked cheeses. A large pricing blackboard lists the cheeses and the flag of origin is pasted next to each. Walnuts fill a basket, wine books abound, and there is a wide variety of salamis, sausages, fruits, chocolates, pates, and fresh sourdough French bread.

If Daryl sounds like an enterprising, hard driving young man, let there be no doubt. He started his first business at age seven and paid his way through college with proceeds from high school ventures. While at San Jose State he had a lettered T-shirt business and when he was getting his master's degree (marketing) at Berkeley he imported and sold wooden clogs.

But a dream he had had since high school days was to resurrect the family winery business. His great grandfather, Vittorio, had founded V. Sattui Winery at his North Beach home in 1885. Later he built a winery in the Mission District at 2505 Bryant Street, where he conducted his wine business until Prohibition forced him to put aside his press for the insurance business.

Daryl, after working at a half dozen north coast wineries to gain a broad range of experience, dusted the cobwebs off his great grandfather's hand corker, brought it north, and with a few school friends and a Nobel physicist for investors, re-founded the V. Sattui Winery just south of St. Helena.

Daryl does most of the work at the winery himself. He says that all of his wines are 100% varietal and that the Cabernet and Zinfandel receive about two years in wood and six months in the bottle before release. "Most of our business is repeat business," he adds. "We'd rather spend our money on the product than on a fancy package or advertising."

Sutter Home Winery

The green building across the highway from the Louis Martini Winery is the Sutter Home Winery. The oldest wooden winery in the valley, the first part of the building was erected in 1874 by the German-Swiss winemaker John Thomann. The structure's sturdiness is attested to by 60 foot beams of 12x16's—part of the 1880 addition—that were (and are) spliced together *without nails*.

Thomann died at the turn of the century and his three daughters sold the winery in 1904 to John Sutter and his son Albert. The Sutters had operated a winery on Howell Mountain since 1890, so they merely moved their inventory and changed the name of the winery to Sutter Home. (John Sutter was a distant cousin of John Augustus Sutter, who built Sutter's Fort and owned the Coloma mill where gold was discovered.)

The winery was used through Prohibition for the production of non-alcoholic grape products, and later leased to a succession of would-be winemakers. The winery's effectual revival began in 1946 when it was purchased by John Trinchero, who had been in the wine business in New Jersey. In 1948 he was joined by his brother Mario.

When John retired in 1960, he sold his interest to Mario and Mario's son, Louis (known as Bob). Bob took over as winemaker and, after a time, began to change the character of the winery. At one time 52 different wines bore the Sutter Home label; Bob had visions of producing but a single wine.

"It all started in the spring of 1968," relates Bob. "Darrell Corti (a Sacramento wine merchant) introduced me to a 1965 Deaver Vineyard (Amador County) Zinfandel made by Charlie Myers (Harbor Winery), then a home winemaker. It was terrific. Two weeks later I had contracted for 20 tons of Ken Deaver's grapes. When our 1968 Deaver Zinfandel hit the market in January of 1971 it was an instant success."

It brought not only success, but direction as well to Sutter Home. The winery will never be a "one wine" winery, as Bob initially envisioned, but it may well become a "one grape" winery. One by one wines were dropped from the Sutter Home list as Zinfandel sales mushroomed. The last holdout is Trinchero's ever-popular Moscato Amabile, a light, fragrant, slightly sweet Muscat wine.

As demand has increased for the Deaver Zinfandels, Trinchero has decided to produce another Zinfandel to take some of the pressure off of the limited production from Deaver's 95 acres. The Deaver Zinfandel will retain the classic black Sutter Home label, while a different Sutter Home label is being designed for the second Zinfandel, the White Zinfandel, and the Moscato Amabile.

Sutter Home is still a family operation. Bob makes the wine, his brother Roger sells it, and the paperwork is handled by their mother, Mary, and Bob's wife Evalyn. And Papa Mario, spry at 80, still sticks his head in the door daily to lend his expertise and guidance wherever needed.

Louis Martini Winery

It's really nothing more than a matter of basic philosophy that the Louis M. Martini Winery has for so long been a leader in selling good wines at reasonable prices. Even now, a quick glance at the Martini price list will show varietals in the $4 range and generics at less than $3 the fifth. "We have a simple pricing policy," says Louis Peter Martini, president and winemaker of the 57-year old corporation. "We just charge what we have to charge to pay our debts and make a little money."

That may sound a little *too* basic, but don't waste your time delving for deeper meanings that don't exist. Like the man himself, it's no facade. The man is large, sturdy, upright and forthright, on the quiet side, and all there. So are the wines.

The beginnings, however, came from a different sort of man. He was Louis Michael Martini, and he was as irascible as Louis Peter is gentle. Blue-eyed, square-jawed, and brimming with the Italian-spiced sauce of life, he loved to bark, "I don't agree with you. And if you agree with me, I'll change my mind!"

Louis the Elder was born on the Italian Riviera in 1887. His father Agostino, a shoemaker by trade, brought his family to San Francisco when Louis was 13. Louis assisted his father in their fish business, but the clams were dying of pollution even then and Agostino looked for another profession.

Louis and his father built a 40 x 75 foot winery behind their Hunter's Point home and made their first wine the fall after the great earthquake. When their first vintage spoiled, Agostino sent Louis back to Italy to study winemaking at the University of Genoa and in Piedmont at Alba. After eight months of intense work, Louis returned to his father and there were no further failures. At one time they had a vineyard and winery between Pleasanton and Sunol. It was in nearby Livermore that Louis Peter Martini was born in 1918.

After gaining broader experience in other wineries, including a stint with Secundo Guasti at Cucamonga, Louis Michael purchased the E.J. Foley Winery (formerly owned by Italian Swiss Colony) at Kingsburg in 1922. That was the start of the L.M. Martini Grape Products Company. One of its most popular products during Prohibition was a grape concentrate for home winemakers tantalizingly called "Forbidden Fruit."

At Repeal Martini looked longingly northward toward an unrealized dream. He knew that great wines could be made in California and his intuition and experience told him that the Napa Valley was the place to go. Without fanfare he built a winery south of the sleepy town of St. Helena that was later called "the most modern and technologically innovative in California." There he made and stockpiled wines until 1940, when he sold the Kingsburg plant, moved his family to St. Helena, and put the whole of his new line on the market at once. It was, in a word, sensational.

At that time Louis the Younger was testing his

Martini's Monte Rosso Vineyards.

wings, both literally and figuratively. He had enrolled at the University of California at Berkeley in 1937, and part of his course work led him to U.C. Davis and specialized studies in enology and viticulture. His degree in 1941 was in Food Technology and he had barely six months of practical experience at the family winery before America was dramatically drawn into World War II.

Louis Peter enlisted in the U.S. Army Air Corps as an aviation cadet, his tour of duty taking him to Great Britain. He left the service a major and returned home to the more peaceable profession of producing and selling wine. In 1947 he married Elizabeth Martinelli. All four of their children were born and raised in St. Helena and the Martinis' home was once the Edge Hill Winery. Built by General Erasmus D. Keyes in 1867, it features two foot thick stone walls.

Louis the Elder turned over winery operations to his son in 1955, but continued to play an active role in the business until his death in 1974. Since that time Louis Peter's two oldest children have joined the family venture. Carolyn, a graduate of Scripps with a master's from Rutgers, is vice president—administration. Michael, a U.C. Davis grad and Air Force vet, is the winery's V.P. for production.

It is a curious point that, in this era of increasingly more specific appellations of origin, the Martinis continue to use the general "California" appellation. Part of their rationale lies in their desire for a broader base of identification and their inclination to blend wines from more than one region. But the primary reason is that the Martini vineyard locations span two North Coast counties, having been chosen for specific attributes and planted to specific varieties.

One of these vineyards is the famed 280 acre Monte Rosso Vineyard, draped splendidly across the thousand foot crest of the Mayacamas Mountains north of Sonoma. Named for its volcanic red earth, the site was first planted to vines in the early 1880's and had been formerly known as Goldstein Vineyard and Mt. Pisgah Vineyard.

The Martinis were among the first to recognize the special viticultural characteristics of the Carneros district south of Napa. They planted vineyards on part of the Stanly estate in 1942 and further expanded their Carneros holdings—entirely with Pinot Noir—in 1964. At 340 acres, it is now the largest of the Martini vineyards. Their other vineyards include benchland along the Russian River, south of Healdsburg, and newer plantings in Chiles Valley, east of Napa Valley toward Lake Berryessa.

Since a bright new tasting room has been built it is no longer possible to taste the many Martini wines over a checked tablecloth in a corner of the cellar, as was once the custom. But it is, on rare occasions, still possible to pick up a bottle of the prized Moscato Amabile, the light, sweet, spritzy wine originally made by Louis the Elder in Kingsburg—by mistake!

Spring Mountain Vineyards

Mike Robbins is one of those rare fortunates who, though cursed with lofty dreams, has been blessed with the ability to fulfill them. An Annapolis graduate engineer who put himself through law school at night, Mike is busily creating a Victorian showplace on the lower reaches of Spring Mountain with all the energy that he used to expend on sizable real estate deals.

An intense man, Robbins made time to learn the art of creating stained glass windows so that his own work would grace his restoration of the elegant Victorian mansion. (The magnificent edifice, modeled after and twice the size of the Beringers' Rhine House, was constructed by Tiburcio Parrott, a prosperous merchant and confidant of both Jacob and Frederick Beringer.) A sensitive man, Robbins had a special kitchen outfitted next to the main kitchen—for the benefit of nearly a dozen hurt and homeless dogs and cats that have been adopted by the Robbins household.

Robbins' Napa Valley odyssey started in 1960 when he was, for a short time, a minor shareholder in Mayacamas Vineyards. In 1962, on a business trip to the valley, his fancy was captured by a stately Victorian home just north of Greystone Cellars. Stately, but in disrepair. The cellar of the vintage 1876 home became a bonded winery in 1968 and two years later

Robbins offered his first wines under the Spring Mountain label.

In 1974 he purchased part of Parrott's Miravalle estate and slowly began to move his operations there. He began building the south wing of his new winery (the fermentation cellar) in 1976, having enough of it completed and outfitted with Mueller fermenters for that year's crush. The main level of the north wing (the barrel cellar), built in front of a 90 foot tunnel dug decades before, was completed early in 1977. This wing will eventually have a second level, where the newest red wines will undergo their malolactic fermentations in barrels before being racked downstairs for their second year of aging in small French oak.

Chuck Ortman, Mike's winemaker of eight vintages, left in January, 1979, to begin a consulting practice. The winemaking chores will now be handled by Bruce Delavan, who has previously worked in both Washington and California wineries.

Robbins has 106 acres of vines in two locations on the eastern side of the valley. Wildwood Ranch, near Rutherford, has primarily Cabernet and Chardonnay, plus a few acres each of Merlot and Cabernet Franc. The smaller Soda Creek Ranch, east of Yountville, is planted to Chardonnay and Pinot Noir.

Land has already been cleared for the first planting of vines next year on the Spring Mountain estate. As the vines come into production Robbins plans to found a new winery, tentatively named Wildwood, based on his two valley vineyards. He is quick to point out that it will be a separate and equal winery and label.

Chateau Chevalier

When Greg Bissonette and his soon-to-be bride Kathy were first looking for a vineyard, they were thinking 15 acres. After camping out one night on the 288 acre Spring Mountain estate that had first been planted by Jacob Beringer, their goals suddenly changed. In 1969, with the help of two partners (since bought out), they purchased the former Chevalier estate and were married in a grove of giant redwoods adjacent to their new winery/home.

The magnificent stone castle was erected by George Chevalier. Modeled after a French chateau near Amboise, the project was completed in 1891. George's father, Fortune, had come from Normandy a stained glass craftsman, but made his fortune selling whiskey and imported wine under his "Castle" brand. His goods were sold in handsome amber bottles with raised glass lettering and a fairy tale castle, complete with turrets and waving pennants.

A family tragedy took the love of the land out of George Chevalier and he sold the estate. Howard Hart owned the property for 25 years, then Leslie Rogers had it for 22 years. Rogers paid no attention to the vineyards, but did devote time to the chateau and its formal gardens. Sadly, after his death the property went to a group of investors who rarely visited their holding. "The vineyards were almost forest again; the gardens were entirely overgrown," remembers Bissonette.

A slender man with a terribly engaging smile, Greg had been a Marine fighter pilot during the Korean War. His father had also been a fighter pilot. "Dad was Toledo's only ace in World War One," recalls Greg. "He even came up against Baron Von Richthofen once."

Greg continued his work as a stockbroker and Kathy took a job with the Department of Mental Health in Napa to sustain the winery early on. Their six children did everything from picking grapes to cleaning up in the winery to help out. Greg's two oldest sons are currently U.C. Davis students. The common effort clearly makes for a cohesive family unit.

The most difficult task was putting in the vineyard. The slopes are steep and the terraces wide. "We have one spot where the tops of the stakes on one row are lower than the bottoms of the stakes on the next row up," marvels Greg. In 1978 a field crushing tank fell off a steep terrace in soft dirt, splashing 600 gallons of precious Chardonnay juice onto the hillside.

Bissonette's wines appear under two labels. Wines made from purchased grapes are bottled under the "Mountainside Vineyards" label. The handsome "Chateau Chevalier" label—featuring the arched stained glass window over the winery's north doorway, framed in black—is reserved for wines produced from the grapes Greg planted and grows on the estate.

Cabernet Sauvignon and Chardonnay are the heart of Chateau Chevalier. Both are bountiful wines, chewy with wood. "When I first started," says Greg, "Louis Martini advised me to make wines I like to drink. I like wines with finesse and oak."

Yverdon Vineyards

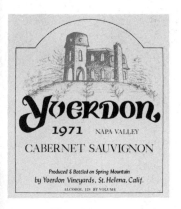

Fred Aves grew up in a small farming town sixty miles west of Chicago. Sent to live with his father in southern California, he attended a polytechnical high school where he was exposed to an eclectic education. Gourmet cooking led to an interest in languages. He liked opera, which prompted him to learn Italian (he speaks five languages), and was an avid skier. Tearing down radios and putting them back together again led to an inventing career.

"I had a 1942 Chrysler, and you couldn't reach the outside mirror from the driver's seat," says Fred. "So I developed a cable controlled mirror, patented it, rented a garage, and I was in the automotive accessories business." Later he developed, patented, and manufactured the curb indicator and exhaust pipe extenders (popularly "headers").

By the late sixties Fred had tired of the automotive business. There was no longer any challenge for him, so he sold his company and looked for new, more sublime horizons. He found them on a forested ridge of Spring Mountain.

"I had been exposed to wine nearly all of my life," he notes. "Three of my four grandparents were from Switzerland and they were all fond of wine. The Eberles (his maternal grandparents) had a village tavern there in Yverdon and I'm sure they made wine. Everybody did."

Aves started making wine in southern California from local grapes, but was disappointed with the results. At first he bought grapes from the Napa Valley, then went ahead and purchased an 80 acre vineyard on Bennett Lane in Calistoga from California wine pioneer Louis Petri. The vineyard, called Rancho Alto, is planted to Cabernet, Napa Gamay, White Riesling, and Chenin Blanc.

In 1969 Fred bought his piece of Spring Mountain and began building "my temple to Dionysus" (the Greek god of wine). When Fred says he is building a winery, he means *he* is building a winery. With his own hands. The two story structure is constructed of hard grade engineer stone and features Tudor arches and quatrefoil stained glass windows. The hardwood paneled walls of an English board room have been restored for the tasting room upstairs and three tunnels will eventually be bored into the hillside from the lower level.

Wines were first produced in 1970. Twelve acres of Gewurztraminer and Merlot were planted below the winery shortly thereafter. Winemaking was suspended for two years (1974 and 1975) while construction of the winery and house was at its peak. The house, of identical stonework, features a cast iron spiral staircase of Fred's design and construction and solid oak and walnut doors hand carved by Fred.

Cathy Corison joined Yverdon as winemaker in January of 1979. A Pomona College graduate in marine biology, she took her master's at U.C. Davis and worked the 1978 crush at Freemark Abbey.

121

Beringer Vineyards

Beringer

Napa Valley
Chardonnay

Produced and bottled by
Beringer Vineyards, St. Helena, Napa Valley, California
Alcohol 12½% by Volume

"Los Hermanos" was the sobriquet given them by their neighbor and longtime friend, Senor Tiburcio Parrott. It survived "The Brothers" to become the trademark of the winery they built more than a hundred years ago.

They were Frederick and Jacob Beringer and they came from a winemaking family in Mainz, on Germany's Rhine River. Frederick was educated in Paris, then sailed to New York in 1866 to start a business as a malt producer. It was this venture that would provide the finances for the winery.

Jacob, five years Frederick's junior, was then learning the cooper's and winemaker's trades in Mainz and Berlin. He, too, came to New York, then moved on to St. Helena in 1872 where he became cellarmaster for Charles Krug. While still in Krug's employ, the popular young man purchased 97 acres called "the old Hudson place" and began planting vines. The year was 1876: America was celebrating its centennial and St. Helena was incorporating.

The following year Jacob hired a hundred Chinese men to begin work on a stone winery. Nearly a thousand feet of tunnels were chiseled out of the mountainside by the coolies, "working with picks and shovels and carrying the debris outside in small woven baskets."

The winery itself was constructed of massive native stone, and measures 40 by 104 feet. The second story was built water tight, caulked regularly, and could be flooded to a depth of several inches without a leak. Grapes were crushed on the third floor, fed by gravity to the second for fermenting, thence to the first floor for barrel aging.

By 1883 the winery was sufficiently established that Frederick could join his brother in St. Helena. His first task was to begin work on a home that would replicate their 17 room ancestral home in Mainz. The foundations and ground floor were cut from native stone and the building framed with California redwood. The wainscottings, staircases, and mantle pieces were of ornately carved white oak ordered from Germany. Intricately patterned floors were cut from oak, mahogany, and walnut. The leaded glass windows were crafted in Europe and eight ornamental fireplaces heated the elaborate house. The Beringers' best friend, Parrott, was so impressed that he ordered the same architect (Herr Schroepfer) to construct an identical mansion for himself a half mile up the hill at his Miravalle estate.

"Uncle Fritz," as Frederick was known to his friends, was active in his adopted community, helping to found the high school, the creamery, and a savings bank. When he died of Bright's disease in 1901, the *St. Helena Star* lauded his "steadfastness to his friends. He was liberal, kindhearted and true, such a man as wins his way into the affections of all."

By the time of his death in 1915, Jacob had purchased the winery interests of Frederick's heirs. A family corporation was then formed by Jacob's children to continue the business. The winery was for many

Oak barrels in Beringer's stone caves.

years headed by Charles Tiburcio Beringer and, after his death, by his sister, Bertha Beringer.

Beringer remained open during Prohibition to produce sacramental and medicinal wines and brandies, giving credence to the winery's claim of being the oldest continuously producing winery in the Napa Valley ("every vintage since 1879"). At Repeal the 600,000 gallon winery employed 36 people and planned to produce 60,000 gallons of dry wine and 90,000 gallons of sweet for their two labels: Los Hermanos Vineyards and Mountain Ranch.

In January of 1971 the sale of Beringer to Nestle, Inc. was completed. The international Swiss food company promptly hired veteran winemaker Myron S. Nightingale Sr. and set aside a substantial amount of money to replant vineyards, replace used cooperage, build a sparkling new production facility (across the highway), and generally re-establish the reputation of Beringer wines.

Today, under the ownership of the Labruyere family of Macon, France, Beringer continues to move forward. A large part of Beringer's resurgence must be attributed to the skill and dedication of Myron Nightingale, who presided over the construction of the modern new winery and has placed great emphasis on the individuality of Beringer's seven vineyard locations.

"All of those involved in the process of winemaking know that premium wines come from superior grapes," says Nightingale. "The quality of that fruit is dependent largely on the combination of soil and climate, but it is the soil which often provides the distinctive character in a glass of premium wine."

Nightingale, a crew-cut, bespectacled scientist, was for 18 years the winemaker at Cresta Blanca. While there, he did pioneering work on botrytised wines, assisted by his wife Alice, which resulted in the renowned Premier Semillon.

The new production facility allows Nightingale the luxury of setting aside small lots of wine from specific vineyards so as to, as he puts it, "nurture a perhaps extraordinary wine which has resulted from special soil conditions."

The southernmost of Beringer's 2000 acres of vineyard are at Big Ranch Road, north of Napa. There 400 acres are planted almost entirely to Pinot Noir and Chardonnay. Two vineyards are near Yountville, one is near Rutherford, and two are at St. Helena. The northernmost vineyard is actually in Sonoma County's Knights Valley, just north of Calistoga. A warm location, this vineyard has shown well with Johannisberg Riesling thus far.

Beringer remains one of the most accessible wineries for visitors, who thrill at the hand-hewn tunnels, the hand-carved oak ovals, and the intricate and intimate tasting room in the glittering jewel that is the Rhine House.

Christian Brothers Winery

As the decade closes The Christian Brothers will mark three hundred years of service. The order was established in France in 1680 by Comte Jean Baptiste de la Salle, a young nobleman who gave up his title to found the Brothers of the Christian Schools (*Fratres Scholarum Christianarum*, or R.S.C.).

The schools provided free education to boys of the working classes. The order was devastated by the French Revolution, but struggled onward. In 1837 the Brothers established their first school on this continent, in Montreal. Eight years later a school was founded in Baltimore, the first in the U.S.

The Christian Brothers first began making wine to support their schools at their original Novitiate in Martinez, possibly in 1879, most certainly by 1882. Their profits then went to nearby St. Mary's College at Moraga, founded there in 1868.

In 1930 the Brothers acquired the Napa property of Oakland business leader Theodore Gier. Gier, who had a thriving winery and vineyard in Livermore (Giersburg), built a three-story stone winery seven miles west of Napa in 1903. Called Sequoia Vineyard and Winery, the property covered 338 acres when the Brothers purchased it. Most was planted to hillside vineyards and the winery held 300,000 gallons of wine.

Within two years the Brothers had erected a new Novitiate and chapel and transferred their operations to the Napa Valley. The site was christened Mont La Salle.

Repeal meant little to The Christian Brothers, except perhaps that their production changed slightly to include dry table wines. But a year later a new cellarmaster arrived at Mont La Salle. He was a gangly, smiling young chemistry teacher by the name of Anthony Diener, and he would lead the Brothers to many a basketball victory against teams from the neighboring wineries. He would also become the world wide symbol of Christian Brothers wines: Brother Timothy.

In 1978 Brother Tim celebrated his Golden Jubilee as a Christian Brother. During the proceedings he spoke of the significance of wine: "Throughout my life I have been fascinated by the fact that the first miracle recorded in the Gospels is the miracle of Cana when Christ 'manifested His glory and His disciples believed in Him.' Converting water into wine directly and instantaneously, He elevated wine and winemaking to a rare position of prominence and prestige. And later, in using wine for the first Eucharist, he gave wine another mark of distinction and a special blessing. For forty-three years it has given me great satisfaction to work with a beverage so blessed by Christ."

In 1945 Christian Brothers acquired the Mt. Tivy Winery at Reedley (Fresno County) for the production of their dessert wines and brandies. Today, half of the winery's profits derive from brandy sales of over a million and a half cases a year. The Christian Brothers, who have been selling brandy since 1940, sell more brandy than any other producer in the country, out-

Mont La Salle Novitiate amidst 200 acres of vines.

selling imports as well.

In 1945 they also began leasing the historic Greystone Cellars in St. Helena, which they purchased five years later. The megalithic winery was erected in 1889 by the altruistic mining magnate William Bowers Bourn Jr. in order to provide independent local growers a place to age wines they could not readily sell.

It took two years and reportedly two million dollars to erect the three story structure. Measuring 80 by 400 feet, with three foot thick stone walls, it was the largest stone winery in the world. The florid pen of Idwal Jones painted this picture: "At St. Helena there were a dozen hale townsmen who remember seeing it rise, block by block, to the yells and sing-song of Chinese masons. But its severe and bleak facade—as of a mews reserved to stable the chargers of horsemen the size of Colossus—and the heroic bulk of it on the plinth of a high terrace, like a pedestal, give it the air of a monument built three centuries ago."

Though Bourn's business sense was sound, he had not taken the phylloxera into account. The building passed through a succession of owners, including Charles Carpy and Cresta Blanca. The California Wine Association, which owned the 3.5 million gallon winery from 1896 to 1926, had the presence of mind to retain the name "Greystone Cellars" for one of their labels. Thus, Christian Brothers must designate the structure as their "North St. Helena Winery."

That distinguishes it from their "South St. Helena Winery," with its magnificent production facility added in 1972. Featuring "fermenting-in-the-round," the facility can efficiently handle a crush of 18,000 tons and ferment three million gallons of wine in any given vintage.

The Greystone winery is now used for sparkling wine production, red wine aging, and as the winery's primary visitor center (visitors are also welcome at Mont La Salle). It also houses and displays much of Brother Timothy's fabulous corkscrew collection, which numbers more than 1400 pieces.

All of The Christian Brothers wines are blends, which vary only in complexity. A Pinot Noir blend with an average age of three years was the result of eight test blends made from 90 samples from four vintages and ten vineyard locations. One Cabernet blend emerged from 134 different lots and several marathon tasting sessions.

These tasting sessions are presided over by Brother Timothy, whose remarkable palate is largely responsible for the notable consistency of Christian Brothers wines from year to year. Since Christian Brothers wines are not vintage dated, Brother Timothy has a full palate of colors to work with to create works of art that reflect the continuity of thought and purpose behind them.

St. Clement Vineyards

The year of the Bicentennial was a banner year for Dr. William J. Casey and his pretty wife Alexandra. Their picture postcard Victorian home celebrated its own centennial and, more importantly, the Caseys crushed their first wines in their miniature basement winery.

The home was built in 1876 by Fritz Rosenbaum of San Francisco. It had been meticulously restored by Mike Robbins after he purchased it in 1962. Six years later Robbins founded Spring Mountain Winery from the cramped stone basement.

When Robbins moved his operations up Spring Mountain to the Parrott Villa, he put the smaller Victorian, situated a half mile north of Greystone Cellars, on the market. By late 1975 he had a buyer, who insisted that some of the 1975 Chardonnay and 1975 Cabernet Sauvignon made there be part of the deal. So St. Clement (accented on the first syllable) had its first wines before its first grapes had been crushed.

Dr. Casey is a Johns Hopkins trained ophthalmologist whose roots run deep in the Maryland soil where his mother's ancestors had settled in the 17th century. Thomas Gerrard, to be specific, was granted St. Clement's Manor by the English crown, sometime after the first English settlement on the Potomac in 1634 by Leonard Calvert, brother to the second Lord Baltimore. The Crossland Cross, embossed in gold on the St. Clement label and atop the lead foil capsule, comes from the Calvert coat of arms (which was later incorporated *in toto* into Maryland's state flag).

After graduation from medical school, Dr. Casey did his internship and residency in San Francisco, then went to Sweden and Jerusalem for successive fellowships, the latter involving corneal transplants. Today Dr. Casey attends his San Francisco practice three and a half days a week—specializing in glaucoma and cataract surgery. The remainder of his time is spent seeing to his winery and the two acres of Cabernet Sauvignon that cascade down the slope to the highway from the house.

"It was Brad Webb who helped get us going in the fall of 1976," recalls Casey. "Later Bob Stemmler and Jon Axhelm assisted me, and now my consultant is Chuck Ortman, who's come full circle. He was the winemaker here for Mike Robbins in the early seventies."

It may be that Ortman's influence will cause Casey to add a third wine to St. Clement's roster of Chardonnay and Cabernet. The experienced winery consultant is fond of Sauvignon Blanc, so the two have been looking for quality growers of that variety. Casey is a strong believer in obtaining grapes from several locales, so much so that he has purchased Chardonnay from as many as nine different growers.

A new, stone-faced fermenting cellar is being built behind the home/winery. Casey hopes to have it completed for the 1979 crush, and will eventually add a wing for office space and additional barrel storage.

Charles Krug Winery

Across the highway from the gigantean Greystone Cellars stands the venerable Charles Krug Winery, today operated by the Peter Mondavi family. During the last century Charles Krug was a progressive leader of Napa Valley's wine industry. One analyst, circa 1881, wrote, "Today he is at the head of the greatest industry in California."

Born Karl Krug in 1825 in Trendelburg, Prussia (now West Germany), Charles emigrated at age 22 to teach in August Glasser's Free Thinkers School in Philadelphia. But in the year Marx and Engels were finishing *Communist Manifesto* (1848) he returned home to participate in a vain attempt to overthrow a reactionary parliament. Krug was imprisoned, but freed shortly thereafter in another outbreak of hostilities.

He returned to the United States to take a job with Jacob Hahnlein as editor of *Staats Zeitung*, the first German newspaper published on the Pacific Coast. In 1854 he quit to farm a government claim at Crystal Springs (San Mateo Co.), not far from Agoston Haraszthy. After eight months, he returned to San Francisco to work in a private gold establishment. He later worked at the U.S. Mint and with Haraszthy.

In 1858 he purchased a small plot in Sonoma from Haraszthy and planted 20 acres of vines. That fall he made 1200 gallons of wine for John Patchett of Napa, using a small cider press borrowed from Haraszthy. It was the first wine pressed in the Napa Valley by means other than Indian feet. (Twenty years later the historic press would be presented to Krug by the then liquidating Buena Vista Vineyard Company. Today it stands proudly in the winery's retail room.)

In December of 1860 Krug married Caroline Bale, the daughter of settler Edward Turner Bale and grandniece of General Mariano Vallejo. Caroline's dowry included a 540 acre ranch in St. Helena. The following spring Krug planted 20 acres to vines, built his first cellar, and made his first wine.

Krug flourished. His winery was a model of neatness and order and his generosity legendary. Said wine historian H.F. Stoll, "He encouraged every newcomer to set out vines and helped them generously with his own time and money to get results." Several great winemakers of the day served their apprenticeships in the cellars of Charles Krug.

Krug was for many years a State Viticultural Commissioner and was the first president of the St. Helena Viticultural Association. His wines were marketed along the eastern seaboard, in Mexico, Germany, and England. Despite his efficient and orderly ways, Krug was to be defeated by the root louse that decimated European and California vineyards alike. When Krug died in 1892 two of his daughters were running the winery and the estate was sadly in debt.

In 1894 Linda and Lolita Krug turned over day to day operations of the winery to their cousin, Bismark Bruck. Bruck produced wine until Prohibition and also produced red grape juice that retailed for $4.50 per case

6000 oak barrels stacked for aging.

of 12 quarts.

At Repeal James K. Moffitt (the paper merchant, banker, and patron of education who was Krug's creditor) leased the vineyards and cellars to Louis Stralla's Napa Wine Company. A decade later Moffitt found the man he adjudged capable of carrying on the Krug tradition. In 1943 he sold the entire ranch to Cesare Mondavi, a calm, serious businessman.

Mondavi, a native of Ancona, Italy, had come to work the iron mines of Minnesota in 1906. After returning to Italy to claim Rosa Grassi for his bride, he returned to Minnesota, where all four of his children were born.

In 1922 Cesare moved his family to Lodi, where he launched a wholesale business in grapes and other fruits. A big part of his business was to supply his friends in Minnesota with grapes for making wine. At Repeal, he began to make wine himself at Acampo.

Satisfied that both his sons were interested in his profession, Cesare acquired the Sunny St. Helena Winery in 1937 to produce dry table wines. Six years later he sold his interest in the Acampo winery and the Sunny St. Helena Winery to purchase Krug for $75,000. Son Robert became the general manager and Peter the winemaker.

Winery and vineyard rehabilitation occupied much of the Mondavis' time and money. When Cesare Mondavi died in 1959 Rosa stepped in to head C. Mondavi & Sons until her death in 1976.

Peter's eldest son, Marc, has since joined the winery. The curly-haired, full-bearded young man will eventually take over most of the business responsibilities. His brother, Peter Jr., is finishing his junior year at Stanford, where he is majoring in mechanical engineering. When he finishes his master's, he will become plant manager.

Peter Mondavi Sr. has always loved the production side of winery management. A Stanford graduate himself, he later spent a semester at U.C. Berkeley researching cold fermentation under Dr. William Vere Cruess, the world-renowned food scientist. He later applied the fruits of that research to winemaking at Charles Krug, the most noticeable result being the famed Krug Chenin Blancs—flowery and moderately sweet.

"To make outstanding wine," says Peter Mondavi Sr., "a vintner should maintain a balance between the introduction of modern equipment and the need to maintain the human element. Old timers believe the quality of a man's wine depends on his own quality and character; a little bit of himself going into every bottle. To gain lasting fame, he has to be a poet, a philosopher, and an honorable man as well as a master craftsman."

Krug fans sign up for *Bottles and Bins*, the delightful newsletter "uncorked and poured from time to time" by Francis "Paco" Gould. Patrons also enjoy the popular August Moon Concerts and Tastings on the Lawn.

Conn Creek Winery

The business name has been changed. What was Conn Creek Vineyards is now Conn Creek Winery. A subtle distinction to some, it reflects a world of difference to Conn Creek's partners.

The seed for Conn Creek was planted in 1967 when Bill and Kathleen Collins purchased the established, head pruned 58 acre vineyard of Alfred Domingos, situated just north of the Old Bale Mill. Shortly thereafter they planted another vineyard just north of Yountville, between the Napa River and Conn Creek.

Bill Collins is a graduate of the Naval Academy and served as a missile submarine officer after World War II. He then went into the electronics business, manufacturing and selling capacitors and telemetry equipment. Living near Palo Alto at the time, Bill and Kathleen became close friends with Stanford professor William Beaver and his wife, May, fellow wine bibbers.

In 1975 Collins and Beaver negotiated the purchase of Hanzell Vineyards, but the deal fell through when legal difficulties arose. The same year Lyncrest Vineyards came on the market. So the two couples leased the former B. Ehlers Winery, acquired the equipment and inventory of Lyncrest, and were even lucky enough to hire Lyncrest's winemaker, John Henderson, who had served an early apprenticeship under Lee Stewart at the original Souverain.

The pinkish stone winery, erected in 1886, had been idle through Prohibition until reactivated in 1932 by Alfred Domingos as the Old Mill Winery. Domingos stayed in business until 1958, from which time the winery again lay empty until 1975. The partners called their enterprise Conn Creek Vineyards, for the Yountville vineyard owned by the Collinses.

This year "Conn Creek" takes on a new meaning for the winemaking corporation, which has as new partners Koerner Rombauer, a Braniff pilot, and his wife Joan. The group has purchased property east of Rutherford, where Highway 128 meets the Silverado Trail. The triangular piece of land, bounded on one side by Conn Creek, will be the site of Conn Creek's new winery.

The new structure will be fashioned after the Collinses' house (of French influence), which was designed by local architect Andrew Batey, a former Rhodes Scholar. The winery will feature a central fermentation area, flanked by two wings, one each for red and white barrel aging.

Conn Creek is gradually shifting its production to eliminate Johannisberg Riesling. In the future Henderson will be concentrating on Chardonnay (from the Yountville vineyard), Cabernet Sauvignon, and Zinfandel (both reds from the Collinses' home vineyard). Chardonnay is expected to represent half of the winery's production of 15,000 cases from the new facility.

Burgess Cellars

The stone and redwood cellars are small. The output is but 20,000 cases per year. There are just 20 acres of venerable vines, mostly Cabernet Sauvignon. But the view from the unpretentious home is exquisite and the history behind the winery lengthy.

The winery and vineyard lie on the lower, western slope of Howell Mountain due north of St. Helena. The winery was part of the original Rossini homestead and was probably built in the early 1880 s, by the grandfather of Marilouise Rossini Kornell.

The vineyards were abandoned through Prohibition, and the then chicken ranch was purchased as a summer home in 1943 by the former Armour Meat Company ad man J. Leland Stewart. Convinced by Bob Mondavi and Andre Tchelistcheff that wine was the way to go, Stewart produced the first wines for his "Souverain" label in 1945. He restored the vineyards, enlarged and remodeled the winery, and commissioned a series of carved wooden doors by artist Merrill Abbot.

In 1970 Stewart "retired" (for thirty days) and sold the winery to an outfit that eventually built a new winery in Rutherford (now Rutherford Hill), and then sold that to Pillsbury. In June of 1972 the Howell Mountain facility and vineyards (but no inventory) were sold to wine buffs Tom and Linda Burgess.

As a youth Tom had visited the old Lonz Winery, which had been founded in 1857 and produced sweet, aromatic Concord wines. (The winery was located on an island in Lake Erie, just offshore from Sandusky, Ohio. It is no longer producing.) But it was the extensive travel that was part of the global missions he flew in the Air Force, and later in his work as a corporate pilot for IBM, that roused Tom's interest in wine. "I had the opportunity to taste wines all over the world," says the lanky Burgess.

The Burgess wines are typically big and intensely varietal. That, Tom will tell you, comes largely from careful vineyard selection. The winery vineyard yields just one quarter of the grapes the winery requires. The remainder come from some of the best independent growers in the Napa Valley. The winery released its first Pinot Noirs last year, one coming from the spectacular Spring Mountain vineyard of Jerome Draper Sr., the other from the Winery Lake Vineyard (Carneros district) of Rene di Rosa. Burgess' complex, dry Chenin Blanc originates in the vineyards of blackberry grower Dick Steltzner.

Burgess' winemaker is Bill Sorenson. While studying wine at Fresno State, the Missouri native was in charge of the school's experimental winery. "Fermenting white wines in oak adds character that you can't get by other methods," says Sorenson. He notes that the Burgess reds are aged in American oak until they complete malolactic fermentation. In the cold stone cellars, the malolactic occasionally has to be helped along by literally draping electric blankets over the small oaken barrels.

Pope Valley Winery

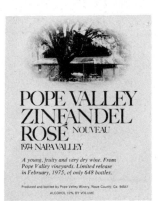

Two miles northwest of the infinitesimal hamlet of Pope Valley is the reborn winery of the same name. Two modest stone pillars flank the entrance, beyond which lies a single acre of crotchety, venerable Semillon vines. They were probably planted some three-quarters of a century ago, shortly before the winery itself was founded.

The redwood timbered winery was built in 1909 by blacksmith Ed Haus. A native of Switzerland, Haus constructed his Burgundy Winery from sturdy timbers salvaged from the nearby Oat Hill quicksilver mine. Thus, the building is buttressed with massive beams and posts, some of which appear to be nothing less than whole trees whose limbs have been smoothly excised.

The building was erected around an excavation into the north-facing shale hillside. The lower level is almost literally a cool shale cave, in which rows of small French and American oak casks patiently mature their vinous contents.

Haus' son and daughter—Sam and Lily—reopened the winery after Prohibition, when it was known as the Sam Haus Winery. Sam, an avid rattlesnake hunter, retired in 1959. The winery was inactive until purchased in 1972 by James and Arlene Devitt.

Arlene and their three small children moved to the winery property to get things underway while Jim commuted from his electronics inventing and manufacturing business in El Segundo.

Devitt's two sons are largely responsible for the successful restoration of the vintage winery. Blond-haired Robert is general manager and is responsible for the books. Winemaker Steve, the older of the two, has already produced some distinctive Zinfandels and Chardonnays.

The pair share a house on the property that Steve says is probably older than the winery. In 1978, with the help of ten of their high school friends (all of whom had become contractors), Bob and Steve poured a 40 x 80 foot concrete pad for their new processing area. Eventually to be roofed over, the pad houses hoppers, a crusher-stemmer, the press, and stainless steel fermenting tanks. It is a vast improvement over the old receiving area that was above the upper level of the main winery, used when the winery was entirely dependent on gravity flow.

Steve says that the probable redefinition of the "Napa Valley" appellation—to include only Napa River watershed land—will have little effect on the winery: "We'll just use 'Pope Valley' for those wines we make from local grapes."

The Devitts are fiercely proud of the family orientation of their venture. Says Arlene, "We worked hard as a family to establish the winery and are grateful for the pride and effort sons Steve and Bob have shown. They are both very talented. Steve, aside from winemaking, plays jazz guitar and is very artistic. Bob plays classical guitar and is our electrician and 'fix anything' person around the winery."

Freemark Abbey Winery

Freemark Abbey, like Franciscan, has never had any connection with the cloistered life, save that its wines have often been dubbed "divine" by connoisseurs. The name actually came to the winery late in its history, derived from the names of the owners who purchased the inactive winery in 1939: Charles *Free*man, *Mark* Foster, and Albert M. Ahern (nicknamed *"Abbey"*).

The situs of the winery had survived a long and variegated history by the time it acquired its religious-sounding name. The first vines were probably planted in 1875 by Captain William J. Sayward, a sea captain who once survived the sinking of his ship in an Atlantic storm without losing a crewman. Sayward, who had purchased the land from Charles Krug, later sold it to John and Josephine Tychson. After her husband died of tuberculosis, Josephine built her Tychson Winery in 1886, perhaps the only winery built by a woman in the century.

Phylloxera forced her to sell the redwood winery, which later came to Antonio Forni, who rechristened it Lombarda Cellars. Forni probably began construction of the present stone structure in 1899, completing it seven years later. He also discovered a distant and untapped market for his wines in the Italian stone masons who quarried marble and granite in Barre, Vermont.

The building had a succession of owners after Prohibition began, until it was revived and renamed by the Aherns of Santa Monica. The Aherns produced a full line of wines and were quite successful with a line of "varietal" jellies.

In 1965 the property was purchased from hotelman Ben Swig by Lester and Barbara Hurd. The Hurds moved their candle factory and retail store into the upper level and two years later leased the lower level to a partnership of growers, who re-established the name and essence of Freemark Abbey.

The group was led by Charles Carpy, whose namesake grandfather had operated the Uncle Sam Wine Cellars in Napa nearly a century ago. Freemark's winemakers, under the guidance of partner/consultant Brad Webb, have produced substantial wines from the beginning. Leon Adams, writing in his first edition of *The Wines of America*, described Freemark's 1968 Cabernet as "the first California red wine I have thus far tasted that I might have mistaken for a good vintage of Chateau Margaux."

In 1973 then-winemaker Jerry Luper created Edelwein, a lush, honeysuckle, *beerenauslese*-styled Johannisberg Riesling that rekindled the interest of California winemakers in late harvested, botrytised Rieslings. Winemaker Larry Langbehn has since followed that act with Rieslings of varying residual sweetness, designated as Sweet Select, Edelwein, and Edelwein Gold (the sweetest).

As special as the botrytised Rieslings are, they should not diminish the winery's solid achievements with Chardonnay, the elegant, Nevers-aged Cabernet Bosche, and the dark, pepperish Petite Sirah.

Stony Hill Vineyards

Two miles up Lyman Canyon Road, between Spring Mountain to the south and Diamond Mountain to the north, is the Stony Hill Vineyard of Eleanor McCrea. The rock-studded hillside, spotted with live oak, boasts about 32 acres of Chardonnay, White Riesling, Gewurztraminer, and Semillon.

Appropriately named, Stony Hill is the creation of Frederick H. and Eleanor W. McCrea. They purchased the property, above the Bothe-Napa Valley State Park, in 1943. Fred, a native of St. Paul, Minnesota, and a graduate of Dartmouth, was then a vice president of the internationally known McCann-Erickson ad agency.

Friends of the McCreas' chided them that the land was good only for goats or grapes. Wanting to make use of their property, they chose grapes. Advice from the University of California suggested Chardonnay for the area, so in 1948 the McCreas began planting five to ten acres a year to vines. Having made small batches of wine in their kitchen, they were encouraged to go on ahead and become winemakers as well. McCrea was one of the first to discard his coat and tie for the rural splendor (and hard work) of winegrowing.

The Stony Hill winery was built and bonded in 1951 and had its first commercial crush the following year. It didn't take long for wine-knowledgeable consumers to beat a path to the McCrea's door, so the wines were made available only through a private mailing list. Though the list has been frozen for more than two years, Eleanor has been forced by short crops during the drought to limit regular customers to but one case apiece.

Despite the spectacular success of his Chardonnays, Fred McCrea remained a friendly, accessible person to aspiring winemakers. A totally unselfish man, he was always willing to share his knowledge with others, typifying the greatest virtue of the winegrowing profession. It was a sad New Year's Day in 1977 when California's wine fraternity was forever deprived of Fred's amiable company.

Stony Hill wines have been made by vineyard and winery manager Michael A. Chelini (Kah-lee-nee) since 1972. Four white wines are produced each vintage. Three — Pinot Chardonnay, White Riesling, and Gewurz Traminer — are sold by Stony Hill under its label, which reads "Grown, produced and bottled 600 feet above the floor of the Napa Valley." The fourth wine is a sweet dessert wine made from Semillon, called Semillon de Soleil, sold only in half bottles from the Corti Brothers stores in Sacramento. Made from grapes dried in the sun on prune-drying trays, the wine usually reaches 13% alcohol and 8% residual sugar.

The small, 7000 gallon winery is filled with older, relatively neutral French and American oak. "We're not that mad about the oak taste," says Eleanor. "The main virtue of oak is that the wine's taste matures earlier."

Kornell Champagne Cellars

The Kornell story is fashioned from a wonderfully varied admixture of ingredients. The primary component, of course, is the champagne master himself, a man bred to sparkling wines as a thoroughbred is to run. Vital to the blend is Marilouise Rossini Kornell, Hanns' wife of over twenty years. The daughter of Napa Valley pioneers, she was educated as a teacher of the physically handicapped, whom she taught for fifteen years, and was for a time a concert lyric soprano. Their marriage has produced two other constituents that are integral parts of Kornell Champagnes: Paula Lisa and Peter Hanns Kornell.

Kornell proudly announces his wine producing heritage on every bottle of wine: "Third Generation Champagnes." Born to a family that had been producing wine since the 1840 s, Hanns will tell you that he was working in his father's wine business at Lublinitz at age four and washing bottles by age five. His plans to take over the family enterprise were thwarted by the imminence of World War II. In 1939 he was interred at Dachau. Conditionally freed, he fled to England until he could make passage to America. He arrived in New York City in August of 1940 with a battered suitcase and two dollars.

He hitchhiked to California and worked for a time at the famed and mysterious Fountaingrove Winery, near Santa Rosa. He then worked for the Gibson Wine Company in Ohio and Kentucky and the American Wine Company in St. Louis. All the while he lived in cheap rooming houses to save money and studied to become an American citizen (which he did in 1946).

In 1952 he returned to California with his savings and a $3000 loan and leased the former Tribuno Winery in Sonoma. There he bottled wine by night and peddled it by day in a battered panel truck. Six years later his dreams began to blossom. When the winery was sold from under him, he moved everything to Larkmead Lane where an old stone winery stood amidst a stand of elms. This was the Larkmead Winery, once owned by the Salmina family, close friends of the Rossinis. The same year he married Marilouise, whose grandfather had planted the vineyard and built the winery on Howell Mountain that became Lee Stewart's original Souverain, and later the cellars of Tom and Linda Burgess.

At Larkmead Kornell continued to produce sparkling wines in the classic *methode champenoise* — same-bottle fermentation. That standard aside, everything from there on is in Hanns' own style. A stocky man possessed of boundless energy, Hanns has never felt tradition-bound to use the classic French varieties, or even to conduct the initial fermentation himself. Instead, Kornell purchases lots of still wines that suit his own particular standards for the production of sparkling wine. Given his upbringing, it is hardly a surprise that White Riesling is responsible for the greater part of his cuvees. Hanns prefers "champagnemaker" to "winemaker," and the fruits of his labor give irrefutable evidence of his skill as a master "champagnemaker."

Schramsberg Vineyards

Schramsberg
FOUNDED 1862

BLANC DE BLANCS

NAPA VALLEY
CHAMPAGNE   VINTAGE 1966

PRODUCED AND BOTTLED BY
SCHRAMSBERG VINEYARDS   ALCOHOL 12% BY VOLUME
CALISTOGA, CALIFORNIA   CONTENTS 4/5 QUART

Napa's first hillside wine-growing estate, Schramsberg lies nearly a mile up the south slope of Diamond Mountain, protected by thickets of redwood, buckeye, and madrone. Though known for fine sparkling wine today, the estate produced only still wines under its founder, Jacob Schram.

A native of Pfeddersheim (on the Rhine, outside of Worms), Schram came to the U.S. in 1842 at age sixteen. Settling in San Francisco, he opened a barber shop and married. In twenty years he had saved enough to buy his piece of Diamond Mountain. His wife Annie supervised the planting of vines while Jacob practiced his tonsorial arts at farms throughout the valley. A solid Victorian home was constructed and 1400 feet of tunnels—Robert Louis Stevenson likened them to bandits' caves—dug into the cool hillside.

Stevenson wrote extensively of his 1880 visit with Jacob and Annie Schram in *Silverado Squatters.* He called the place "the picture of prosperity" sitting "among the tangled wildwood" where the sunlight, vines, and bottles of maturing wine "made a pleasant music for the mind."

Schram's wines graced the wine lists of San Francisco's elegant Palace Hotel and London's esteemed Charlton Clubs. His table wines sold for $5 per case of quarts in 1895, while his Sauterne commanded the princely price of $7 the case.

When Schram died in 1905 his son Herman inherited the estate. At the onset of Prohibition it was sold to an investment firm, thence in 1921 to Captain Raymond Naylor. Two subsequent owners—John Gagano and Douglas Pringle—replanted vineyards and produced sparkling wines for a time.

The inactive winegrowing estate was rescued in 1965 by Jack and Jamie Davies. A native of Cincinnati, Jack was raised in Southern California and educated at Stanford and Harvard. Formerly a management consultant for large industrial companies, he also brought a sense of aesthetics to the wine life. His goal at Schramsberg is to produce "Methode Champenoise sparkling wines of individual quality which display an aged characteristic." He adds frankly, "We have not achieved that yet." If not, he is awfully close.

During the last six years he has been holding back twice as much bottled wine for aging as was being sold. He has now reached what he calls "equilibrium": an inventory of 800,000 bottles of wine that repose on the yeast for two and a half to three years each.

Schramsberg is known for its Blanc de Blancs, a blend primarily of Chardonnay and Pinot Blanc. Says Davies, "The objective is a relatively light bodied, dry, vinous wine that will be appealing as an aperitif or with light seafoods and white meats. The dosage is low (about .75 residual sugar) and includes the use of both old wine and cognac to add to the complexity and style. It develops best at five to six years from vintage and one year from disgorging."

A popular specialty is the Schramsberg Cremant, a dessert styled sparkler with just half the bubbles.

Stonegate Winery

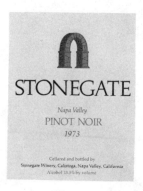

STONEGATE

Napa Valley
PINOT NOIR
1973

Cellared and bottled by
Stonegate Winery, Calistoga, Napa Valley, California
Alcohol 13.5% by volume

Jim and Barbara Spaulding cut their winegrowing teeth fighting raccoons and birds in the frozen suburbs of Milwaukee, where Jim was for twenty years a medical science writer for the *Milwaukee Journal*. They had 40 vines of differing denominations, including Baco Noir, Marechal Foch (French hybrids), and White Riesling from the New York State experiment station at Geneva and Pinor Noir and Cabernet Sauvignon from U.C. Davis. "We had to fence the entire vineyard, including the top, to protect against the raccoons," recalls Jim. "Then, once the grapes had any sugar, we had to put paper bags over the clusters to protect them from the birds!"

In 1969 Jim took a year's leave of absence and came west to teach journalism at the Berkeley campus of the University of California. During that visit he purchased a piece of hillside property west of Calistoga that had "prunes and walnuts and old grape stakes" on it. In 1971 the Spauldings made the westward move a permanent one, Jim resumed his professorship at Berkeley, and 15 acres of rootstock were put in at the Kortum Canyon Road property.

Two years later they started their winery with Paul Landeros, who had prunes at the corner of Highway 29 and Dunaweal Lane, just below the then-new Sterling Winery. Their 1973 vintage was crushed and fermented at Burgess while a small frame farm building was refitted for wine production. In 1975 the Spauldings bought Landeros' interest in Stonegate. (The name, incidentally, was Barbara's creation, associating wine with rocky soil and stone wineries. Also, there is a stone wall around the hillside property.)

The prunes had long since given way to the 15 acres of Pinot Noir, Chardonnay, and Sauvignon Blanc surrounding the olive-hued winery. They complement the like acreage of Cabernet Sauvignon, Merlot, and Chardonnay that had been budded at the hillside vineyard.

The winery is run on a day to day basis by the Spauldings' son David, who makes the wines along with Michael Fallow. Fallow, who has a master's degree in viticulture from Davis, is also responsible for the vineyards. Barbara is usually at the winery two days during the week to keep up with the bookkeeping and Jim joins the crew on weekends and during the summer. "I like the pruning and other stuff," says Jim, "but there's such a glut of governmental forms."

David, a lean, bespectacled fellow whose bookcase implies an eclectic education, has been quietly creating an inventory of substantial wines. While the general thought is that the winery will eventually specialize in Cabernet Sauvignon and Sauvignon Blanc, it would be difficult to convince their patrons that the Stonegate Chardonnays should be put aside. I particularly recall their buttery, fleshy 1976 Sonoma offering and the more recent vanillin-laced, smokey/oaky 1977 vintage from their hillside vineyard. Wines with such character cannot be summarily dismissed.

Sterling Vineyards

STERLING VINEYARDS

Napa Valley Table Wine
PINOT CHARDONNAY
Grown, Produced and Bottled by Sterling Vineyards.
Calistoga-Napa Valley-California

Just south of Larkmead Lane the highway swings left on a wide arc and the upper end of the valley spreads out before you. Framed by a sweeping vista of vines is a wooded knoll that rises 250 feet above the flat valley floor. Atop this eagle's lair looms an imposingly austere white structure, reminiscent of a Tibetan monastery or an Aegean island fortress. In its simplicity it dominates the landscape. Smart, straight lines give way only to the gentle curves of the bell towers.

This sparkling white showplace is the home of Sterling Vineyards, a venture begun in 1964 by four principals of Sterling International, the San Francisco based paper company. Vineyards were planted, with careful attention to matching variety to soil and climate. In 1968, well before winery development had begun, Sterling hired Richard W. "Ric" Forman as winemaker.

His first order of business was to advise the winery builders of his needs as a winemaker. Whatever was needed, whatever the cost, the winery was to have. The result is a thoroughly modern, intelligently laid out physical plant, graced with ceramic tile mosaics in the floors and stained glass windows that bathe the cellars with prismatic rays of daylight.

Sterling's first wines were made in 1969 in temporary quarters at the foot of the hill. From the start they exhibited thoughtfulness. Merlot was employed extensively to soften Forman's Cabernet Sauvignons, which were fined with egg whites and bottled from small French oak. (Merlot has also been made as a varietal since 1972.) A dry, austere Chenin Blanc of great character boasted thirty percent Chardonnay in its composition.

In 1977 Sterling was purchased by Coca Cola of Atlanta. The winery's second label was abolished and generic production halted. The wine list is being pared to but four wines (made only from Sterling's own vineyards): Cabernet, Merlot, Chardonnay, and Sauvignon Blanc. "We intend to make Sterling America's great chateau, a gem," promises Albert E. Killeen, the head of Coca Cola's wine operations. "Although we have purchased two new prime vineyards for Sterling production will be strictly limited to no more than 90,000 cases."

Change continued in 1979 as Ric Forman departed to found his own winery with Peter Newton, an original partner in Sterling. Forman's post has been filled by Theo Rosenbrand, Beaulieu's cellarmaster of more than two decades, and Sergio Traverso, formerly of Domaine Chandon. In March, ground was broken for a two story barrel cellar that will hold 1300 oak barrels. Modeled after a Bordeaux *chai*, Sterling's Reserve Cabernet and Reserve Merlot will each rest there for two years prior to bottling.

Sterling remains a prime tourist attraction with its colorful aerial tram cars, the carillon chimes, its panoply of tasting terraces and rooms, and Sterling's gracious and knowledgeable hosts.

Cuvaison

CUVAISON
1976
Napa Valley
Chardonnay

Alcohol 13.1% by Volume
Produced and bottled by Cuvaison, Inc., Calistoga, California

Cuvaison was founded in 1970 by a pair of scientists from San Jose, Tom Cottrell and Tom Parkhill. The venture was a struggle and Parkhill withdrew after little more than a year. Cottrell carried on, making a wide variety of wines in a quartet of stainless steel fermenters huddled against the hillside, under the cover of friendly oaks. Once fermented, the wines were barrel aged in a former farmhouse that is charitably described as "rustic."

In 1974 the winery was rebuilt from the ground up when the Corporation Trust Company of New York bought in. A handsome, mission-styled winery—cream white with a red tiled roof—was completed in June, 1974. A small retail room was built in the same style just below the winery and an oak-shaded patio is equipped with picnic tables for visitors.

The crowning change, however, came with the selection of a highly talented winemaker whose broad scope of experience had covered four continents.

A native of Switzerland, Philip Ivor Togni brought both an academic and a practical background to Cuvaison. A graduate of London's Imperial College of Science, Togni studied at Montpellier before taking a degree in enology from the University of Bordeaux. He had also done research work at the University of Chile and worked in Algeria, Margaux (Ch. Lascombes), and Alsace (House of Hugel) before coming to California.

Once here he worked in the Napa Valley at Mayacamas and Inglenook. He helped found Chalone in 1960, spent three years in "Varietal Studies" research at Gallo, and for seven years played an important role in the establishment of Chappellet's winery and vineyards.

In 1975 he was hired to give a new direction to Cuvaison. He wasted little time in reducing the multitude of wines produced to three and ordering the grapes from winery-owned vineyards sold off. A strong proponent of hillside-grown grapes, Togni spends a significant amount of his time tramping through the Napa Valley, scouting for the best Cabernet, Zinfandel, and Chardonnay vineyards. "A good winemaker has one foot in the vineyard and the other in the winery," he says. And does. In fact the only vineyard the winery now claims is the one acre of Cabernet growing in front of the winery, on a gentle slope.

Much publicity was garnered by Cuvaison a couple of years ago when it released a substantial Cabernet Sauvignon grown in Marin County, perhaps the first and only Cabernet ever made from Marin County grapes. But that unique wine should not detract from the superb Napa Valley wines Togni has created, all of which are richly-bodied and subtly spiced from their rest in French oak.

Cuvaison sits on a rise along the Silverado Trail just south of Calistoga. Its name, by the way, is French for the length of time red wines are fermented on their skins.

Diamond Creek Vineyards

When Al Brounstein tired of the frantic pace of owning and running Standard Drug Distributors in Los Angeles, he decided to become a winegrower. In 1967 he purchased 79 acres on Diamond Mountain and began planting grapes the following year. In 1969 he and Boots (his wife) moved to San Francisco, where Al learned the marketing of wine by working for Stuart Imports, Sebastiani, Weibel, and Anchor Distributing.

Assisted by his consultant, Jerry Luper, Al produced the first vintage of Diamond Creek wine in 1972.

The key to understanding Diamond Creek lies in the vineyard. There are actually three vineyards, each distinguished by its soil type. The largest vineyard is in blanched, light volcanic soil, and is called Volcanic Hill. The iron-rich soils of Red Rock Terrace produce prolific vines that yield soft, more readily drinkable wines. The smallest vineyard is Gravelly Meadow, so named for obvious reasons.

Each vineyard is planted primarily to Cabernet Sauvignon; in each, Merlot and a smattering of Malbec and Cabernet Franc are interplanted. Though Merlot comprises 6% of the vines, it accounts for 10% of the wines.

The wines are fermented in open-topped, 500 gallon redwood tanks situated at the base of the three vineyards and shaded only by a roof of fibreglass. Says the blue-eyed six-footer, "I love making wine in the vineyard. What could be more appropriate?"

Diamond Creek produces only Cabernet Sauvignon and the wines from each vineyard are bottled separately under the vineyard designation. Aged in Nevers oak, they are neither fined nor filtered. Brounstein expects to market 2000 cases in 1980 when, he says, the winery will show its first profit.

When Al was starting out, Andre Tchelistcheff suggested that the volcanic section would produce the best Cabernet. Louis Martini observed that his best Cabernets had come from the red earth of his Monte Rosso Vineyard. Vineyardist Dick Steltzner voted for Gravelly Meadow. The buoyant but diplomatic Brounstein agrees with all of them!

Brounstein's marketing technique is unique. He invites customers and retailers to one of a dozen picnics each summer. These are held just above the vineyards, where the Brounsteins have created a woodland lake by damming Diamond Creek. Swimming and boating follow a picnic lunch, a vineyard tour, and informal tastings and discussion.

In 1978 Al and Boots moved into an airy, split level redwood home just below the vineyards. The garage serves as a temporary aging cellar. The Brounsteins plan to begin excavation for their permanent winery (storage and bottling) in 1980. Faced with stone, it will be tucked into the hill at the apex of Red Rock Terrace. Later, a new residence will be constructed atop the winery and the present home will become a guest house for winery visitors.

Chateau Montelena

A solitary, pine-covered hillock stands at the base of the hulking Mt. St. Helena, where mountain streams form the headwaters of the Napa River. Atop the rise one discovers an interesting juxtaposition of architectural philosophies: against the hillside is a stone winery of last century's French Chateau style; just beyond is a five acre lake, the nucleus of an oriental park replete with red lacquered pavilions, weeping willows that move with the breeze, and a dragon-eyed five ton Chinese junk.

The address is Tubbs Lane. The winery is Chateau Montelena, founded in 1882 by whaling tycoon Alfred Tubbs. A native of New England, Tubbs had come to San Francisco in 1850, there establishing a cordage factory (producing rope for ship rigging). Once a state senator, Tubbs purchased the 275 acre estate, due north of Calistoga, in 1880. Two years later he had the fortress-like winery notched snugly into the hillside. Designed by a French architect, the rear and sides are of native stone, the front of imported cut stone.

In 1886 Tubbs sailed to France. He brought back vine cuttings and a French winemaker, one Jerome Bardot, who was lauded for the vintages he produced.

Yort Frank acquired the estate in 1958. A Chinese engineer, it was he who contributed the second architectural mode. (In 1964 the estate's mansion—called Hillcrest and built by Alfred Tubbs—burned to the ground.)

Four years later the estate was sold to Lee Paschich, who planted seventy acres to Cabernet Sauvignon and Zinfandel. In 1972 he brought in partners James Barrett and Ernest Hahn, hired Croatian winemaker Miljenko "Mike" Grgich, and Chateau Montelena was on the winemaking map again.

It was decided that only four wines would be produced. They chose what they felt were California's two best reds and two best whites: Cabernet Sauvignon, Zinfandel, Chardonnay, and Johannisberg Riesling.

Grgich didn't let his partners down, producing a rich, creamy Chardonnay his first time down the track. His second Chardonnay brought international recognition to Montelena when it won the much-publicized Paris tasting in May of 1976.

Montelena has been fortunate with winemakers. When Grgich left in 1977 to start his own winery, the partnership was lucky enough to obtain the services of Jerry Luper, recently returned from a European sabbatical. Luper had begun his enological training at age eighteen, taking samples and washing glassware at the E. & J. Gallo Winery in Modesto. He later worked in the analytical lab and participated on the tasting panel for the research department. A slender man with a full, dark beard, Luper's Napa Valley reputation was secured forever when he produced the honied delight "Edelwein" when he was Freemark Abbey's winemaker. It was the first time a rich botrytised wine had been produced commercially in the warm, dry climate of the valley.

Other Wineries

Alatera was originally to have been named for Father Jose Altimira. Unfortunately, it was discovered that another winery owned rights to the priestly pioneer's name.

The equally euphonious "Alatera" was eventually picked for its phonetic likeness to *a la terra*, meaning "from the earth." The winery's stockholder/growers consider the name symbolic of their attention to the soil and their recognition of the importance of grape quality to fine wine production.

The enterprise was founded in 1977 by Bruce M. Newlan, a former Lockheed physicist who had planted Cabernet Sauvignon at the present winery site in 1968, and Holbrook T. Mitchell, a longtime grape grower and home winemaker near Healdsburg. Their first wine is called "1977 Paradis de Napa Valley Pinot Noir." *Paradis* means paradise in French, but in Beaujolais refers to white wines made from the crushed free run juice of black grapes (before pressing). At Alatera, this white Pinot Noir was aged in French and Yugoslavian puncheons and is dry, yet complex with fruit and oak.

Alatera is operating out of a converted farm building, but the owners have plans to build a permanent winery at the end of Hoffman Lane.

BUEHLER VINEYARDS

A tiny, tastefully designed winery and 60 acres of vines overlook Lake Hennessey (to the south) from a Conn Valley hillside. Most of the vines are head pruned, to limit production and increase quality. That the quality is here is amply attested to by the stature of those who buy the grapes: Burgess, Cuvaison, and Chateau St. Jean.

The property is owned by West Pointer John P. Buehler Sr., who retired a full Colonel from the Army and then put in another twenty years with the Bechtel Corporation in San Francisco. His son, John P. Buehler Jr., is vineyardist and winemaker. They produced 800 cases of Cabernet Sauvignon and Zinfandel from their first crush in 1978, both of which have deep color and chewy tannins in their prepubescence.

John Jr. plans to add Pinot Blanc to his repertoire. "There was already a glut of Chardonnay when we bought the property in 1973," says Buehler Jr. "So we planted ten acres to Pinot Blanc. Nine dollars a bottle for California Chardonnay is outrageous, so I think there will be a demand for what I call 'poor man's Burgundy.'"

The 650 square foot winery, crammed with small oak, is in the basement of a small building next to the home of John Jr. and his wife Lisa. An office is upstairs, where a deck overlooks vineyards and valley.

The principals of this fledgling winery are all third generation members of Napa Valley families. Winemaker Mike Forni is the grandson of pioneer grape grower Charles Forni, whose cousin Anton built Lombarda Cellars (now Freemark Abbey).

Jim and Paul Cassayre (the "e" is silent) and Mike Forni are University of Santa Clara trained civil engineers. Forni joined the brothers' company, Cassayre & Associates, after spending four years with the nuclear energy division of General Electric. All three had been amateur winemakers and the engineering firm had been involved in several winery design projects, some of which include Carneros Creek, Rutherford Vintners, Mt. Veeder, and Stag's Leap.

Their own winery saw first light of day when they helped crush their Cabernet Sauvignon at Carneros Creek in 1976. Rich with eucalyptus and wood character, it encouraged further effort. Since 1977 their wines have been made out of a timeworn red barn behind Forni's home.

Cassayre-Forni has no vines. "We believe in obtaining the best grapes from regions noted for distinctive wines of that variety," says Forni. Thus, their Zinfandel grapes hail from Sonoma (Dry Creek) and Amador counties, their Cabernet from the Rutherford and Stag's Leap districts, and their dry, but fruity Chenin Blanc from near Napa.

GREEN & RED VINEYARD

Jay Heminway just wanted to get out of the city when he bought a steep piece of hillside land above Chiles Creek in 1970. His first priority was to make the cold-water-only hunter's cabin livable. After that he ran cattle for a short time.

Before his escape to the country Heminway had been a multi-media sculptor. He had taught at U.C. Berkeley, then worked with the Hansen-Fuller Gallery in San Francisco. He had also spent a year working in the vineyards and cellars of Chateau Lascombes in Bordeaux.

Impressed by the 1968 Zinfandels of Sutter Home and Mayacamas, when Heminway decided to plant vines he chose Zinfandel over Cabernet. He planted four acres in 1972 and added another three in 1977. All are cordon pruned for better air circulation and even ripening.

Heminway's winery is a wooden barn that he converted. The interior walls are a bright, cheery yellow, lighting up a few dozen oak casks, an open redwood fermenter, and two stainless steel tanks. Jay made 300 cases in 1977, his first crush, and 730 cases in 1978. He'll feel comfortable doing about 1500 cases a year when his vines are mature.

Heminway is assisted by wine consultant Larry Wara. Green & Red's 1978 vintage, tasted out of wood, exhibited a soft peppercorn nose and a hint of herbaciousness.

Jay is now considering planting other varieties that might be compatible with Zinfandel.

Keenan

PINOT NOIR
1977 Napa Valley

Produced and Bottled by ROBERT KEENAN WINERY
SPRING MTN, ST. HELENA, CA, Alcohol 13.4% by Volume

In the fall of 1974 Robert Keenan purchased 190 acres along the northeast slopes of Spring Mountain that had once been a home to grape vines. Pine and madrone forest had reclaimed the land, but the empty stone shell of the winery built in 1904 by Peter Conradi still stood.

The slopes below the winery were cleared and Cabernet Sauvignon and Chardonnay vines began life anew. In 1977 the sturdy stone structure was transformed into a spacious modern winery. A solid fir gantry in the center of the building supports a sweeping loft/deck that is connected to the office and lab on the second level. Spanish-coopered French oak barrels and stainless steel fermenters line the inside walls on the ground level.

The same year 51 tons, mostly Chardonnay, were crushed under the direction of winemaker Joe Cafaro. A Fresno State graduate, Cafaro spent two years at Charles Krug before his six year stint at Chappellet. For three years there he worked under Philip Togni, then was head winemaker for his last three years. His initial efforts at Keenan are impressive.

Keenan has been in the insurance business in San Francisco during the thirty years since his graduation from Stanford. He is now retiring from that business to build a home near the winery and devote his energies to his new venture.

LONG VINEYARDS

The vines, in deep, rocky soil, overlook Conn Valley and Lake Hennessey to the north, and the Napa Valley proper beyond. A yellow frame house with white trim stands nearby, built in the 1920's by farmer Karl Frankenstein. The dwelling is now a period piece, tastefully furnished with polished-wood antiques from generations of Longs.

Robert B Long Sr., a property manager and real estate investor, bought this Pritchard Hill property in 1965 as a summer home. The following two years saw 10 acres of Johannisberg Riesling and 5 acres of Chardonnay planted there by Long's son **and** daughter-in-law: Bob and Zelma Long.

Zelma, of course, has been an enologist at Robert Mondavi for a decade. Bob, like his father, was once in property management. Now he is so busy tending vines and wines and building his winery that he has little time for his bird watching, a hobby well-suited to the forested hillocks above Conn Valley.

The Longs produced their first wine, a 1977 Chardonnay, at Trefethen Vineyards. Their first crush in their own small facility came in 1978, when 1100 cases of Riesling and Chardonnay were made. "We really wanted to make a Moselle-styled Riesling," says Bob, "but Mother Nature wouldn't let us. We get fantastic sugars and acids up here." Thus the resulting wine has 10% alcohol, 9% residual sugar, and exhibits peach-like fruit that is well balanced with acid.

Four 60,000 gallon steel tanks used to stand as the frontispiece of the old St. Helena Cooperative Winery (later operated by United Vintners). The giant tanks have been removed by new owner H. Bruce Markham, exposing the stone facade of the original winery, erected in 1876.

The former Rocky Mountain ad man began acquiring vineyard land in 1975, when he bought a 75 acre vineyard in Calistoga. He has since added vineyards at Yountville and just north of Napa on West Oak Knoll. In 1978 he took over the million gallon winery and began remodeling the dilapidated plant. Nearly 200,000 gallons of open-topped redwood fermenters have been dismantled, two of the three crushing lines have been completely reworked, and a tiled, sterile bottling room has been built.

Managing the operation and making Markham's varietal wines is Bryan Del Bondio, whose father has long been associated with Inglenook. The red-bearded Davis graduate was born just two miles from the winery he now oversees.

The cannon piece and soldier on the Markham label may confuse until you learn that Markham was a gunnery officer in the Navy and his father an artillery officer in the Army. The winery will not be heavily fortified.

Don Charles Ross crushed 15 tons of Sauvignon Blanc from two Lake County vineyards in 1978. It was the first crush for Ross' Napa Vintners, though the company had been in existence two years. Ross had previously purchased lots of Cabernet Sauvignon and Zinfandel for his "N V Wines" label. He plans to crush about 40 tons of Sauvignon Blanc, Cabernet, Petite Sirah, Chardonnay, and possibly Chenin Blanc this year.

Having no vineyards, Ross believes in crediting the growers for their part of the winegrowing process. "I'm proud to endorse the vineyards our wines come from on the label because we know that the quality of the wine is determined by the quality of the grapes," he says.

The great grandson and grandson of Napa Valley winemakers (both at Inglenook), Ross is a former Porsche mechanic who turned to winemaking for the challenge. "There are few places today where quality is as appreciated as it is in the wine business. There are so many facets to the wine business that you can't get bored."

Ross' 5000 gallon winery takes up one bay of the Chrisoula Building, part of a small industrial complex only blocks from downtown Napa.

NIEBAUM-COPPOLA ESTATES

Gustave Niebaum's mansion and carriage house stand in the shadow of Mount St. John at the end of Niebaum Lane. The lovely old carriage house, with its twin cupolas, has been converted into a 10,000 gallon winery by the estate's present owner, film director ("The Godfather") Francis Ford Coppola. (The estate was once owned by the John Daniel family, and later by the van Loben Sels of Oakville Vineyards.)

It is Coppola's intention to produce just two estate bottled wines, which will carry the "Niebaum-Coppola Estate" label, plus the federally required "Red Table Wine" or "White Table Wine." The red will be a blend of Cabernet Sauvignon, Cabernet Franc, and Merlot; the white is to be Chardonnay.

The winery's first crush was conducted in 1978 by winemaker Russ Turner, who once sold supplies and grapes to home winemakers in Los Angeles. An accountant by training, Russ served his winemaking apprenticeship at Mayacamas. He plans to bin his wines in a small stone cave (near the winery) that was excavated in 1882.

The estate presently has 110 acres in vines. Zinfandel, Charbono, and Cabernet Sauvignon predominate, and most of the grapes are still sold to Inglenook. The eight acres of Cabernet Franc were increased to twenty-six in 1976, when an additional twenty-five acres of Cabernet Sauvignon were also planted.

Robert Pecota wants to encourage local talent, so his label will display a different piece of four-color art work with each vintage. His 1978 label frames an engaging Ken Wilkens watercolor of a grape vine in full leaf. This year's label boasts a Zelma Stevens oil painting of California Golden Poppies, awash with bright, warm oranges and yellows.

Pecota is the youngest of eleven children born to his Russian immigrant parents. His dairyman-turned-evangelist father was a "connoisseur of all foods," according to Bob. "He forced us to taste foods of all nationalities."

After an education in economics, Pecota put his taste buds to work as a buyer in the aromatics industry of coffees and teas, working eleven years for Hills Brothers and MJB. His friendship with H. Robert Bras, then the head of Nestle's Coffee and Tea Division, turned into a job as grape buyer when Nestle bought Beringer and Bras became its president.

Pecota still spends two or three days a week at Beringer. The remainder of his time is devoted to enlarging the small winery adjacent to his home and replanting his 38 acre vineyard. Much of his effort will be concentrated on Petite Sirah. He has already gone to some lengths to select a desirable clone.

QUAIL RIDGE

He is a slight, slender man, bearded, with a voice that is cavernously resonant. As it happens, he expects to age his wines in a Silverado Trail cavern, originally dug as a quicksilver mine, later a source of bootleg brandy.

Jesse Corallo started life intending to become a CPA, later a lawyer. World War II scuttled those plans, turning him instead into a fighter pilot. He flew 129 missions in P-38s over the South Pacific.

The war over, he went into real estate subdivision before turning to television, then in its infancy. In time he became a free-lance production manager, responsible for the organization of motion pictures, commercials, and documentaries. Between jobs he made Cabernet Sauvignons and Chardonnays at his Brentwood home. When his wines came to the attention of writer John Movius and Spring Mountain's Mike Robbins, they encouraged him to turn professional.

In 1976 Jesse moved to the Napa Valley to do just that. The following year he found his Mount Veeder property, built a house, and laid plans for a vineyard of about 20 acres (primarily Chardonnay). While Jesse still takes on assignments from Hollywood, it may be that his mission in life is to produce richly fruited Chardonnays. His first commercial lot was crushed in 1978 at nearby Vose Vineyards, where it was fermented in Limousin oak barrels. Thick with fruit and vanillin, it is a wine that is at once fleshy and crisp on the palate.

Pete Minor practiced dentistry for twelve years in Berkeley, where he had studied zoology as an undergraduate. During that period he spent an increasingly larger part of his week working a piece of land atop Spring Mountain. He cleared sections of the fir, madrone, and oak forest for four acres of Cabernet and Merlot and constructed a cozy fieldstone home, to which he is now adding a tower.

In 1974 Pete dug an "L" shaped tunnel into a north facing slope and bonded his winery, producing only Cabernet Sauvignon that year. Since then he has also made two vintages of Chardonnay and a single botrytised Johannisberg Riesling. The Riesling came from an Atlas Peak vineyard that has since, been torn out.

Like his vines, Minor seems to thrive on the clean mountain air. Satisfied that they can do well along the crest of the Mayacamas chain, he is ready to plant three acres to Chardonnay and Johannisberg Riesling. He may even add some Gewurztraminer.

The headwaters of Ritchie Creek, which flows through Bothe-Napa Valley State Park to the Napa River below, form on Minor's 48 acre property. The Ritchie Creek label was designed by Pete's wife Maggie.

Napa Valley
Gewürztraminer
1977
Round Hill

Alcohol 12.0% by volume
Produced and bottled by Round Hill Vineyards, Rutherford, California

The Round Hill label covers wines that are crushed at the winery, wines that are custom-crushed elsewhere, and wines that are purchased. All have represented excellent value. But the essence of Round Hill is the cherubic, ebullient Charles Abela, a mechanic - turned - winery - builder.

The label was introduced in 1976 by retailer Ernie Van Asperen, who then sold it to Abela, a former marine mechanic. Abela's first wines were purchased from wineries that had more wine than they could sell. The following year Abela leased the former winery building behind The Arbor complex on Lodi Lane and began refitting it. The structure, crammed with stainless-steel and French oak, was inaugurated with a crush of 216 tons in 1978. Another 180 tons were crushed for Abela at Rutherford Hill.

Abela's thick, strong hands gesture as he talks about his winery. "I got into this as a semi-retirement," he says. "I figured it would require about three days a week, and then I would have plenty of time for hunting and fishing. As it is, I've never worked so hard in my life. But I feel good."

Round Hill's new winemaker is Doug Manning, who spent over four years in the cellars at Joseph Phelps. Abela, who has no vineyards, hopes than once the facility is completed he can spend more of his energy on marketing, hunting, and fishing.

ST. HELENA WINE COMPANY

The St. Helena Wine Company began life with its 1978 crush of 27 tons of Cabernet Sauvignon and Merlot from three Napa Valley vineyards. "We try to purchase grapes from selected rows within selected vineyards," says president Dan Duckhorn. "There's a great risk in trying to buy that selectively, without long term contracts, but I feel that it's the only logical way to go."

Duckhorn, a wine industry consultant, formerly operated Vineyard Technical Services and Vineyard Consulting Corporation at the winery's 11 acre site (the corner of Lodi Lane and the Silverado Trail).

Duckhorn, a wine industry consultant, formerly operated Vineyard Technical Services and Vineyard Consulting Corporation at the winery's 11 acre site (the corner of Lodi Lane and the Silverado Trail). Duckhorn's winemaker is Thomas Rinaldi, who previously toiled at Franciscan and Round Hill wineries. Jerry Watarida is cellarmaster.

Dan and Margaret Duckhorn hope to produce classic Bordeaux styled wines by means of traditional Bordeaux methods. They even went so far as to procure glass barrel bungs. In addition to Cabernet and Merlot, the Duckhorns plan to add one or more white wines. A Graves-styled Sauvignon Blanc is one likelihood.

"We don't want chewy, heavy wines," says Dan Duckhorn. "We're looking for a lighter, more elegant style of wine. Seventy-five percent of any wine is in the grape, so our primary goal is to find the best grapes we can."

"There's some magic in a one-wine winery," enthuses Justin Meyer. Producing Cabernet Sauvignon and nothing but Cabernet Sauvignon, Silver Oak is a sort of a magical, dream winery to Meyer, a strong advocate of California Cabernets. It has to be a little dream-like, because the facility itself is nothing more fancy than the old Oakville Dairy (the wines are fermented at Franciscan). But it's what comes out of the bottle that counts, and what comes out of Silver Oak bottles is 100% Alexander Valley Cabernet from the Los Amigos Vineyard of partner Ray Duncan (who also owns Franciscan Vineyards with Justin). About 4000 cases are produced each year and the bottles are finished with a sparkling silver label.

Silver Oak Cabernets are aged about two years in new American oak and two years in the bottle before their release in January of the "fifth" year. The wines tend to be fleshy, with broad flavors and noticeable oak. Meyer notes that the deep, fertile soils in the Alexander Valley cause the wines to be naturally soft, precluding the necessity of softening them with Merlot.

Silver Oak's 1974 North Coast Cabernet Sauvignon was released in January 1979 at ten dollars the fifth. A gold medal winner at the Los Angeles County Fair, the wine is soft, its fruit expansive. The grapes were harvested in mid-October at 23.2 Brix, and both alcohol and acid are on the low side.

Nearly forty acres of vines cover the hills and dales of Smith-Madrone Vineyards, 1700 feet up on Spring Mountain. Three-quarters of the acreage is planted to equal amounts of Cabernet Sauvignon and Chardonnay, which will ultimately be the winery's primary wines. The remaining vines are Johannisberg Riesling and Pinot Noir.

The 200 acre hillside property was purchased in 1971 by Stuart and Susan Smith. They immediately began clearing the land of brush and old grape stakes; the first vines were planted the following year. Soon thereafter they were joined by Stu's brother Charles, who had been teaching school in the Bay area.

In 1974 they began construction of a stone and redwood winery building that, when completed, will have a couple of interesting features. A small underground barrel cellar has already been dug under the ground floor, but there are plans for an extension back into the hill. Sometime this year Stu and Susan hope to begin building their residence atop the center portion of the winery, with thick sod steps following the winery roofline down on both north and south sides.

With their first crush in 1977 the Smiths concentrated on whites, producing just 50 cases of Chardonnay and 250 cases of a delightful Johannisberg. A small amount of Cabernet was added with the 1978 crush and Pinot Noir will be made in 1979.

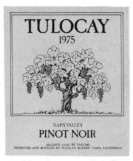

Tulocay's two crisply clean, whitewashed buildings—once part of a chicken ranch—rest atop a sharp rise, up the hill from the Silverado Junior High School and up the road from the 120 year old Tulocay Cemetery.

Raised in Oakland, William Charles "Bill" Cadman was a specialist stockbroker on the floor of the Pacific Stock Exchange in San Francisco when he decided to chuck it all for a simpler form of life. During the crush of 1971 he took a job operating the crusher at Charles Krug. After that he spent 18 months learning from Joe Heitz ("an invaluable experience"), a crush each for Clos Du Val and United Vintners, and then crushed grapes for himself (9 tons) in 1975.

Bill and Barbara Cadman outfitted their minuscule winery by obtaining used equipment from wherever they could get it. A bottle filler came from Pepsi Cola, an air conditioner from a meat packing house, a used crusher from Carneros Creek, and temperature-controlled stainless steel fermenters from a dairy. But they drew the line at oak cooperage. In that case it was nothing but new French and American white oak.

Tulocay's label, with its grape-laden vine, made its debut in October of 1978.

Hamilton Vose III foresees increasing potential for the exportation of American wines. He also considers Zinfandel the closest thing to being California's indigenous wine grape. Thus, it is no surprise that Zinfandel plays a large part in Vose's plans. He's even come up with a proprietary name for his white Zinfandel: Zinblanca.

"I knew that Mt. Veeder would grow good Zinfandel," says Vose. "In looking toward the export market, I decided that a slightly sweet white Zinfandel would be most suitable. A friend of mine—Susan Burns—and I sat around the fire one night trying out words that sounded good phonetically, yet also gave a clue to the wine's identity. That's how we came up with Zinblanca."

The former Chicago businessman has 90 acres of his Mt. Veeder property planted to Cabernet Sauvignon, Chardonnay, and Zinfandel. Further plantings will increase the acreage to around 200.

Cabernet Sauvignon and white Zinfandel were crushed for Vose's label in 1977 at Napa Wine Cellars. Last year he crushed all three varieties at his own winery, an insulated Butler building that is handsomely faced with native stone.

The Aging Caves at Schramsberg Cellars.

Appendix

ALATERA VINEYARDS, INC. Page 160
    Address: 5225 St. Helena Hwy., Napa
    Phone: (707) 944-2914
    Hours: no specifically established
    Facilities: tasting and tours
    Winemaker: Bruce Newlan; Holbrook Mitchell
    Vineyards: approx. 60 acres
    Volume: 2,000 cases annually

BEAULIEU VINEYARD Page 85
    Address: 1960 St. Helena Hwy., Rutherford
    Phone: (707) 963-3671
    Hours: 10-4 daily
    Facilities: tours, tasting, sales
    Winemaker: Tom Selfridge
    Vineyards: 745 acres
    Volume: 245,000 cases annually

JOHN BECKETT CELLARS Page 61
    Address: 1055 Atlas Peak Rd., Napa
    Phone: (707) 224-2022
    Hours: none
    Facilities: not open to the public
    Winemaker: John Beckett & Phil Baxter
    Vineyards: 150 acres
    Volume: 4,000 cases annually

BERINGER WINERY Page 123
    Address: 2000 Main Street, St. Helena
    Phone: (707) 963-7115
    Hours: 9:30 to 4:30 daily
    Facilities: tasting, tours, sales, gift shop
    Winemaker: Myron S. Nightingale Sr.
    Vineyards: 2,800 acres
    Volume: 200,000 cases annually

BUEHLER VINEYARDS Page 160
    Address: 820 Greenfield Rd., St. Helena
    Phone: (707) 963-2155
    Hours: none
    Facilities: not open to the public
    Winemaker: John Buehler Jr.
    Vineyards: 60 acres
    Volume: 800 cases annually

BURGESS CELLARS Page 139
    Address: 1108 Deer Park Rd., St. Helena
    Phone: (707) 963-4766
    Hours: 10-4 daily
    Facilities: sales; tours by appointment
    Winemaker: Bill Sorenson
    Vineyards: 20 acres
    Volume: 20,000 cases annually

CAKEBREAD CELLARS Page 79
    Address: 8300 St. Helena Hwy., Rutherford
    Phone: (415) 835-WINE; (707) 963-9182
    Hours: by appointment only
    Facilities: tours and sales by appointment only
    Winemaker: Bruce Cakebread
    Vineyards: 20 acres
    Volume: 10,000 cases annually

CARNEROS CREEK WINERY Page 53
    Address: 1285 Dealy Lane, Napa
    Phone: (707) 226-3279
    Hours: Mon.-Fri. 10-4
    Facilities: sales; tours by appointment only
    Winemaker: Francis Mahoney
    Vineyards: 30 acres
    Volume: 13,000 cases annually

CASSAYRE-FORNI CELLARS Page 161
    Address: 1271 Manley Lane, Rutherford
    Phone: (707) 944-2165 or 255-0909
    Hours: limited
    Facilities: tasting, tours, sales by appointment
    Winemaker: Mike Forni
    Vineyards: none
    Volume: 3,000 cases annually

CAYMUS VINEYARDS Page 89
    Address: 8700 Conn Creek Rd., Rutherford
    Phone: (707) 963-4204
    Hours: by appointment only
    Facilities: sales & tasting by appointment only
    Winemaker: Randall Dunn
    Vineyards: 70 acres
    Volume: 15,000 cases annually

CHAPPELLET VINEYARDS Page 93
    Address: 1581 Sage Canyon Rd., St. Helena
    Phone: (707) 963-7136
    Hours: no tours or tasting
    Facilities: sales by mailing list
    Winemaker: Anthony M. Soter
    Vineyards: 95 acres & grapes from nearby vnyds
    Volume: 25,000 cases annually

CHATEAU CHEVALIER WINERY Page 119
    Address: 3101 Spring Mt. Rd., Box 991, St. Helena
    Phone: (707) 963-2342
    Hours: by appointment only
    Facilities: advance appointment only
    Winemaker: Gregory Bissonette
    Vineyards: 60 acres plus purchased grapes
    Volume: 65,000 cases annually

CHATEAU MONTELENA Page 159
    Address: 1429 Tubbs Lane, Calistoga
    Phone: (707) 942-5105
    Hours: 10 to 4, Monday-Friday
    Facilities: retail sales, tours by appointment
    Winemaker: Jerry Luper
    Vineyards: 70 acres plus purchased grapes
    Volume: 20,000 cases annually

THE CHRISTIAN BROTHERS WINERY Page 127
    Address: 2555 North Main St., St. Helena
    Phone: (707) 963-2719
    Hours: 10 to 4, daily
    Facilities: tours, tasting, sales
    Winemaker: Brother Timothy
    Vineyards: 2,400 acres
    Volume: (storage - 20,000,000 g.)

CLOS DU VAL Page 63
Address: 5330 Silverado Trail, Napa
Phone: (707) 252-6711
Hours: 9 to 4, weekdays
Facilities: sales; tours by appointment
Winemaker: Bernard M. Portet
Vineyards: 120 acres
Volume: 15,000-18,000 cases annually

CONN CREEK WINERY Page 137
Address: 3222 Ehlers Lane, St. Helena
Phone: (707) 963-3945 or 963-9100
Hours: by appointment only
Facilities: sales and tours by appointment
Winemaker: John Henderson
Vineyards: 112 acres
Volume: 15,000-16,000 cases annually

CUVAISON Page 155
Address: 4550 Silverado Trail, Calistoga
Phone: (707) 942-6266
Hours: 10 to 4, Thurs.-Mon.
Facilities: sales
Winemaker: Philip Togni
Vineyards: 1 acre
Volume: 20,000 cases annually

DIAMOND CREEK VINEYARDS Page 157
Address: 1500 Diamond Mountain Rd., Calistoga
Phone: (707) 942-6926
Hours: no visitor accommodations
Facilities: group tours & picnics by appt. only
Winemaker: Albert Brounstein
Vineyards: 20 acres
Volume: 2,000 cases annually

DOMAINE CHANDON Page 69
Address: California Dr., Yountville
Phone: (707) 944-8844 (off); 944-2280 (visitors)
Hours: 11 to 6, Wed.-Sun.
Facilities: tasting ($1.50), tours, sales, restaurant
Winemaker: Edmond Maudière
Vineyards: 900 acres (half planted as of 1978)
Volume: 50,000 cases (sparkling) annually

FRANCISCAN VINEYARDS Page 101
Address: 1178 Galleron Rd., St. Helena
Phone: (707) 963-7111
Hours: 10 to 6 daily
Facilities: tasting, tours, sales, gifts
Winemaker: Justin Meyer
Vineyards: 900 acres
Volume: 80,000 cases annually

FREEMARK ABBEY WINERY Page 143
Address: 3022 St. Helena Hwy., St. Helena
Phone: (707) 963-9694
Hours: 10:30 to 4:30 daily
Facilities: tours (at 2 p.m. daily), sales, gifts
Winemaker: Larry Langbehn
Vineyards: 130 acres
Volume: 24,000 cases annually

GREEN AND RED VINEYARD Page 161
Address: 3208 Chiles Pope Valley Rd., St. Helena
Phone:
Hours: not open to the public
Facilities: no visitors please
Winemaker: Jay Heminway
Vineyards: 7 acres
Volume: 1,500 cases projected

GRGICH HILLS CELLARS Page 97
Address: 1829 St. Helena Hwy., Rutherford
Phone: (707) 963-2784
Hours: by appointment only
Facilities: by appointment only
Winemaker: Miljenko "Mike" Grgich
Vineyards: 140 acres
Volume: 10,000 cases annually

HEITZ WINE CELLARS Page 107
Address: 500 Taplin Rd., St. Helena
Phone: (707) 963-3542
Hours: 11-4:30 at 436 St. Helena Hwy. South
Facilities: tasting Mon.-Fri.; sales daily
Winemaker: Joe & David Heitz
Vineyards: 50 acres
Volume: 40,000 cases annually

INGLENOOK VINEYARDS Page 81
Address: St. Helena Hwy., Rutherford
Phone: (707) 963-7184
Hours: 9-5 daily
Facilities: tasting, tours, sales, wine-related gifts
Winemaker: Thomas A. Ferrell
Vineyards: 2,800 acres
Volume: 4,500,000 cases annually

ROBERT KEENAN WINERY Page 162
Address: 3660 Spring Mtn. Rd., St. Helena
Phone: (707) 963-9177
Hours: 8 to 4:30
Facilities: sales; tours by appointment
Winemaker: Joe Cafaro
Vineyards: 48 acres
Volume: 7,000 cases annually

HANNS KORNELL CHAMPAGNE CELLARS Page 147
Address: 1091 Larkmead Lane, St. Helena
Phone: (707) 963-2334
Hours: 10 to 4 daily
Facilities: tasting, tours, sales, gifts
Winemaker: Hanns Kornell
Vineyards: none
Volume: 100,000 cases annually

CHARLES KRUG WINERY Page 133
Address: 2800 Main St., St. Helena
Phone: (707) 963-2761
Hours: 10 to 4 daily
Facilities: tours, tasting, sales
Winemaker: Peter Mondavi
Vineyards: 1,200 acres
Volume: 1,500,000 cases annually

LONG VINEYARDS Page 162
Address: Box 50, St. Helena
Phone: (707) 963-2496
Hours: not open to the public
Facilities: none
Winemaker: Zelma & Bob Long
Vineyards: 15 acres
Volume: 1,500 cases annually (2,000-2,400 proj.)

MARKHAM WINERY Page 163
Address: 2812 N. St. Helena Hwy., St. Helena
Phone: (707) 963-9577
Hours: Wed. - Sun.
Facilities: tasting and sales (subject to change)
Winemaker: Bryan A. Del Bondio
Vineyards: 264 acres
Volume: 9,200 cases annually

LOUIS M. MARTINI Page 113
    Address: 254 St. Helena Hwy. So., St. Helena
    Phone: (707) 963-2736
    Hours: 10 to 4:30 daily
    Facilities: tasting, tours, sales
    Winemaker: Louis P. Martini & Michael R. Martini
    Vineyards: 800 acres
    Volume: 320,000 cases annually

MAYACAMAS VINEYARDS Page 57
    Address: 1155 Lokoya Rd., Napa
    Phone: (707) 224-4030
    Hours: by appointment
    Facilities: tours & sales by appointment only
    Winemaker: Bob Travers
    Vineyards: 45 acres
    Volume: 5,000 cases annually

ROBERT MONDAVI WINERY Page 75
    Address: 7801 St. Helena Hwy., Oakville
    Phone: (707) 963-9611
    Hours: 10:30 to 5 daily
    Facilities: tasting, tours, sales
    Winemaker: Robert & Tim Mondavi
    Vineyards: 1094 acres
    Volume: 850,000 cases annually

MT. VEEDER WINERY Page 55
    Address: 1999 Mt. Veeder Rd., Napa
    Phone: (707) 224-4039
    Hours: none
    Facilities: tours on weekdays by prior appointment
    Winemaker: Michael A. Bernstein
    Vineyards: 20 acres
    Volume: 4,500 cases annually

NAPA VINTNERS Page 163
    Address: 1721 C Action Ave., Napa
    Phone: (707) 255-9463
    Hours: by appointment only
    Facilities: sales by appointment
    Winemaker: Don Charles Ross
    Vineyards: none
    Volume: 2,100 cases annually

NAPA WINE CELLARS Page 71
    Address: 7481 St. Helena Hwy., Oakville
    Phone: none yet
    Hours: by appointment only
    Facilities: retail sales
    Winemaker: Charles Woods
    Vineyards: 3 acres
    Volume: 10,000 cases annually

NICHELINI VINEYARDS Page 95
    Address: Highway 128, St. Helena
    Phone: (707) 963-3357
    Hours: 10 to 6 weekends
    Facilities: tasting, tours, sales, picnics
    Winemaker: James E. Nichelini Sr.
    Vineyards: 160 acres
    Volume: 6,000 cases

NIEBAUM-COPPOLA ESTATES Page 164
    Address: 1460 Niebaum Lane, Rutherford
    Phone: (707) 963-9435
    Hours: none
    Facilities: tours by appointment only
    Winemaker: Russ Turner
    Vineyards: 110 acres
    Volume: 2,000 cases

ROBERT PECOTA WINERY Page 164
Address: 3299 Bennett Lane, Calistoga
Phone: (707) 942-6625
Hours: none
Facilities: by appointment only
Winemaker: Bob Pecota
Vineyards: 35 acres
Volume: 1,500 cases annually

JOSEPH PHELPS VINEYARDS Page 105
Address: 200 Taplin Rd., Box 1031, St. Helena
Phone: (707) 963-2745
Hours: T-F by appt.; Sat. 10-4:30 by advance res.
Facilities: tasting, tours, & sales by appt.
Winemaker: Walter Schug
Vineyards: 154 acres
Volume: 40,000 cases

POPE VALLEY WINERY Page 141
Address: 6613 Pope Valley Rd., Pope Valley
Phone: (707) 965-2192
Hours: 11 to 5 Sat. & Sun.; by appt during week
Facilities: tasting, sales
Winemaker: Steve Devitt
Vineyards: 1 acre
Volume: 12,000 cases annually

QUAIL RIDGE Page 165
Address: 3230 Mt. Veeder Rd., Napa
Phone: (707) 944-8128
Hours: none
Facilities: not open to the public
Winemaker: Jesse Corallo
Vineyards: none yet
Volume: 700 cases annually

RAYMOND VINEYARD AND CELLAR Page 103
Address: 849 Zinfandel Lane, St. Helena
Phone: (707) 963-3141
Hours: by prearranged appointment only
Facilities: tasting, tours, sales by appt only
Winemaker: Walter Raymond
Vineyards: 80 acres
Volume: 20,000 cases annually

RITCHIE CREEK VINEYARD Page 165
Address: 4024 Spring Mtn. Rd., St. Helena
Phone: (707) 963-4661
Hours: by appointment only
Facilities: tasting, tours, sales by appt only
Winemaker: Pete Minor
Vineyards: 6 acres
Volume: 400 cases annually

ROUND HILL WINERY Page 166
Address: 1097 Lodi Lane, St. Helena
Phone: (707) 963-2228
Hours: by appt only
Facilities: none available
Winemaker: Doug Manning
Vineyards: none
Volume: 33,000 cases annually

RUTHERFORD HILL WINERY Page 91
Address: P.O. Box 410, St. Helena
Phone: (707) 963-9694
Hours: only 10 to 4 on 2nd Sat. of every month
Facilities: tasting, tours, sales
Winemaker: Phil Baxter
Vineyards: none
Volume: 35,000 cases annually

RUTHERFORD VINTNERS Page 99
    Address: 1673 St. Helena Hwy. South, Rutherford
    Phone: (707) 963-4117
    Hours: 10 to 4:30 daily
    Facilities: tasting, sales, gifts
    Winemaker: Bernard L. Skoda
    Vineyards: 30 acres
    Volume: 15,000-20,000 cases annually

ST. CLEMENT VINEYARDS Page 131
    Address: 2867 St. Helena Hwy. North, St. Helena
    Phone: (707) 963-7221 or (415) 421-1866)
    Hours: by appointment only
    Facilities: sales
    Winemaker: William J. Casey & Chuck Ortman
    Vineyards: 2 acres
    Volume: ultimate 6,000 cases annually

ST. HELENA WINE CO. Page 166
    Address: 3027 Silverado Trail, St. Helena
    Phone: (707) 963-7108
    Hours: not open yet
    Facilities: sales
    Winemaker: Thomas Rinaldi
    Vineyards: none
    Volume: 1,500-2,000 cases annually

V. SATTUI WINERY Page 109
    Address: White Lane, St. Helena
    Phone: (707) 963-7774
    Hours: 9:30 to 5:30 daily
    Facilities: tasting, sales, cheese shop, picnicking
    Winemaker: Daryl Sattui
    Vineyards: none
    Volume: 3,500 cases annually

SCHRAMSBERG VINEYARDS Page 149
    Address: Schramsberg Rd., Calistoga
    Phone: (707) 942-4558
    Hours: by appointment
    Facilities: tours, sales
    Winemaker: Harold Osborne
    Vineyards: 40 acres
    Volume: 20,000 cases annually

SILVER OAK CELLARS Page 167
    Address: 915 Oakville Cross Rd., Oakville
    Phone: (707) 944-8866
    Hours: not open to the public
    Facilities: sales at Franciscan Vineyards
    Winemaker: Justin Meyer
    Vineyards: see Franciscan
    Volume: 4,000 cases annually

SMITH-MADRONE VINEYARDS Page 167
    Address: 4022 Spring Mtn. Rd., St. Helena
    Phone: (707) 963-2283
    Hours: by appointment only
    Facilities: tours & sales
    Winemaker: Charles, Stuart, Susan Smith
    Vineyards: 38 + acres
    Volume: projected 5,000 cases annually

SPRING MOUNTAIN VINEYARDS Page 117
    Address: 2805 Spring Mtn. Rd., St. Helena
    Phone: (707) 963-4341
    Hours: by appointment only
    Facilities: none available to the public
    Winemaker: Bruce Delavan
    Vineyards: 106 acres
    Volume: 16,000 cases annually

STAG'S LEAP WINE CELLARS Page 65
  Address: 5766 Silverado Trail, Napa
  Phone: (707) 944-2020 or 944-2782
  Hours: by appointment only
  Facilities: tours, sales
  Winemaker: Warren Winiarski
  Vineyards: 44 acres
  Volume: 15,000 cases annually

STAGS' LEAP WINERY Page 67
  Address: 6150 Silverado Trail, Napa
  Phone: (707) 944-2792
  Hours: by appointment only
  Facilities: none available to the public
  Winemaker: Carl Doumani
  Vineyards: 100 acres
  Volume: 9,000 cases annually

STERLING VINEYARDS Page 153
  Address: 1111 Dunaweal Lane, Calistoga
  Phone: (707) 942-5151
  Hours: 10:30-5 daily, summer; 10:30-4:30, winter
  Facilities: tasting, self-guided tours, sales
  Winemaker: Theo Rosenbrand
  Vineyards: 350 acres
  Volume: 85,000 cases annually

STONEGATE WINERY Page 151
  Address: 1183 Dunaweal Lane, Calistoga
  Phone: (707) 942-6500
  Hours: 10 to 4 for sales weekdays
  Facilities: tours by appointment
  Winemaker: David Spaulding
  Vineyards: 30 acres
  Volume: 8,000 cases annually

STONY HILL VINEYARD Page 145
  Address: P.O. Box 308, St. Helena
  Phone: (707) 963-2636
  Hours: by appointment only
  Facilities: tours by appt. only. (No Sales)
  Winemaker: Michael Chelini
  Vineyards: 30+ acres
  Volume: 3,000 cases annually

SUTTER HOME WINERY, INC. Page 111
  Address: 277 St. Helena Hwy. South, St. Helena
  Phone: (707) 963-3104
  Hours: 9 to 5 daily
  Facilities: tasting and sales
  Winemaker: Louis (Bob) Trinchero
  Vineyards: none
  Volume: 36,000 cases annually

TREFETHEN VINEYARDS Page 59
  Address: 1160 Oak Knoll Ave., Napa
  Phone: (707) 255-7700
  Hours: by appointment only
  Facilities: by appointment only
  Winemaker: David Whitehouse & John Trefethen
  Vineyards: 550 acres
  Volume: 20,000 cases annually

TULOCAY WINERY Page 168
  Address: 1426 Coombsville Rd., Napa
  Phone: (707) 255-4699
  Hours: not open to the public
  Facilities: none available
  Winemaker: W. C. Cadman
  Vineyards: none
  Volume: 1,000 cases annually

VILLA MT. EDEN Page 73
    Address: P.O. Box 147, Oakville
    Phone: (707) 944-8431
    Hours: by appointment only
    Facilities: by appointment only
    Winemaker: Nils Venge
    Vineyards: 83 acres
    Volume: 6,500 cases annually

VOSE VINEYARDS Page 168
    Address: 4035 Mt. Veeder Rd., Napa
    Phone: (707) 944-2254
    Hours: not open to the public
    Facilities: none available
    Winemaker: Hamilton Vose III
    Vineyards: 90 acres
    Volume: 3,000 cases annually

YVERDON VINEYARDS Page 121
    Address: 3787 Spring Mtn. Rd., St. Helena
    Phone: (707) 963-4270
    Hours: not open to the public
    Facilities: none available
    Winemaker: Cathy Corison
    Vineyards: 92 acres
    Volume: 5,000 cases annually

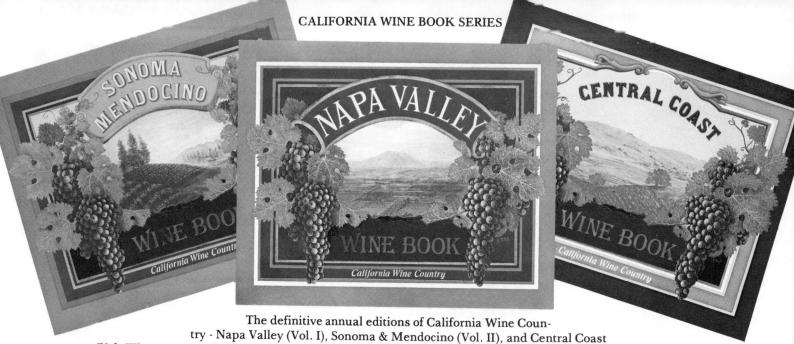

The definitive annual editions of California Wine Country - Napa Valley (Vol. I), Sonoma & Mendocino (Vol. II), and Central Coast (Vol. III) are now available! Absolutely up to date and all inclusive, the Wine Book Series explores every existing winery in the coastal wine growing regions from Mendocino to Santa Barbara. Each handsome 7¼ x 9 inch volume is extensively illustrated with lithographs by famed California artist Sebastian Titus. Special emphasis has been given to the colorful and sometimes enigmatic winemakers and their wines. Each edition contains detailed area maps pinpointing exact winery locations and a complete appendix providing easy reference to vital information. $6.95 per volume

WINE TOUR GUIDE SERIES

For those fortunate enough to visit California's wine growing regions, we offer the "Wine Tour" Series. These three books covering the regions Napa Valley, Sonoma & Mendocino, & the Central Coast are companions to our "Wine Book" Series. These are complete guidebooks for the wine traveler with a chapter on FOOD which reviews noteworthy restaurants and

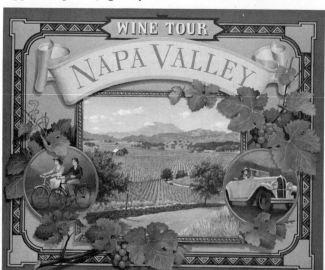

for picnickers, a listing of local shops purveying provisions. A chapter on LODGING reviews the best inns, resorts & campgrounds. Included are many detailed road maps and points of interest. The WINERY chapter lists all the relevant information such as address, phone number, hours, facilities and includes specific directions on how to get there. These are the only books of their kind and are a must for the wine country traveler. $2.95 each